PAWS FOR A MINUTE

Inger Martens

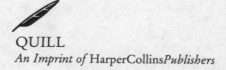

QUILL
An Imprint of HarperCollinsPublishers

...his book is dedicated to my father, who taught me that when prepa-
ation meets opportunity, that's success. And to my mom, whose
unconditional love guided me to believe in myself and to believe that
dreams can come true.

HarperCollins books may be purchased for educational, business, or sales
promotional use. For information please write: Special Markets Department,
HarperCollins Publishers Inc., 10 East 53rd Street, New York, NY 10022.

FIRST EDITION

Designed by Kellan Peck

Library of Congress Cataloging-in-Publication Data
Martens, Inger.
Paws for a minute : people training for dog owners / Inger Martens—1st ed.
p. cm.
ISBN 0-380-80478-6
1. Dogs—Training. 2. Dogs—Behavior. 3. Dog owners—Psychology. I. Title.
SF431.M46 2000
636.7'0887—dc21   00–029692

00 01 02 03 04 RRD 10 9 8 7 6 5 4 3 2

"Inger's tips made it easy to apply Wyatt's training to our lifestyle. Her approach is unique and she's the best there is."
KEVIN COSTNER

•

"We have the highest praise for Inger's gift as a dog trainer. She's equally good with our five-pound Maltese as she is with a German Shepherd. She has a viable solution to every behavior problem that I ever presented her with. My dog comes on command and I've yet to see a little toy breed as well mannered as mine."
DR. LESLIE PAM, psychologist

•

"When my two dogs were growling and attacking my clients at work, I was desperate. Inger trained me how to behave and solved the problem. My aggressive behavior toward my dogs' misbehavior was the issue. Now I'm a better and more calm dog owner and my dogs are saints. Inger deserves all the credit."
JOHN CORSER, commercial director

•

"Working with Inger was extremely beneficial, enlightening, and complete. She will make just about anyone a better dog owner and every dog a better animal."
NANCY GILTNER, K-Cal Channel 9

•

"Inger's terrific and teaches everything really simply, which has given us great results with our dog Momo!"
ALAN ROSENBERG, actor, *Cybill*

•

"I had a seven-year-old dog who knew nothing. Thanks to Inger, I now have a dog who can teach me a few new tricks!"
LEILA KENZLE, actress, *Mad About You*

•

"I consider Inger to be in the upper echelon of animal behaviorists/trainers in America. She is considerate, honorable, dedicated, and very compassionate. Her training protocols effect great success and our clients endorse her highly."
JOHN B. WINTERS, M.S., D.V.M., Beverly Hills Small Animal Hospital

CONTENTS

Acknowledgments

It is a gift to truly enjoy what you do for a living. Therefore I am blessed.

What inspired me to write this book was my discovery of the many humorous human habits that we have as dog owners and that our dogs unconditionally endure. It became my mission to train the dog owners, and thanks to those human quirks and an endless amount of encouragement from my clients, I was able to write this book. Thank you to all of my students throughout the years, people and pooches.

A special thank you to Dusty Hunter for all of her tireless love and support, and for being the best fairy dogmother there is.

I thank Stefan Klima for countless hours of assistance and Chinese food, from the beginning of the process to the end. And for allowing Bo to help you overcome your fear of German shepherds.

My thanks to my agent, Kim Witherspoon, for believing in my concept with such confidence, and to her incredible staff. A special thanks to Josh Greenhut for giving me such support and for having the patience of a saint through the book's development.

Jonathan Exley, thanks for your amazing photography and true friendship. And for rescuing Lily, the wonder dog, off the freeway. Without her I would not have met you.

Kevin Costner, your kindness and generosity make the world a nicer place. I thank you from the bottom of my heart. Soraya Delawari, thank you for your support and for returning my calls right away.

To J. D. Souther and Baby Girl, thank you for being photographed for my book and letting Miss Daisy swim in your cement pond. Thanks to Mr. Murphy for keeping Bo in line as a guest in your house.

Leila Kenzle, you are a very special person. Thank you for your incredible friendship and unconditional support and for helping me prove that you can teach an old dog new tricks.

Thank you to Alan Rosenberg and Marg Helgenberger for your devoted support and for owning Momo, a canine whom I have known for many lifetimes.

Thanks to the Norton family: Peter, Eileen, Diana, and Michael—and, of course, the coolest standard poodle, their Daisy.

An enormous thank-you to LeAnn Rimes, Raven, and Belinda.

Beverly Walton, Jon Barris, Mary Merchant, and Nancy Pachter, you are my true cheerleaders. Thank you for your enthusiasm and support.

To Leslie Pam and Ann Christie, thank you for getting Dolly and enlightening my life.

A very special thank-you to Karen Herek for allowing me into your dog obedience class for adults when I was twelve years old.

A huge thanks to Chris Condrey, Janet Fletcher, Sarah Durand, Jenny Good, and Avon Books for seeing my vision and making me the happiest person on the planet.

Preface

Hocus Pocus Focus.
Believe in Yourself.
You Can Do It.

Over twenty years of teaching clients, I have learned that people hate to train their dogs. They just want them to behave. Dog training is often misunderstood to be discipline or tedious drilling to fix bad behavior. The end result is that the dog just doesn't get trained. Observing this, I realized that training has to be taught with humor, adding entertainment to education.

Training should be a fun way of bonding with your dog. The truth is that the process of training your dog is a lot easier than getting a raise from your boss. Just as in other personal relationships, creating a friendship with your dog takes a little chemistry, some elbow grease, and an understanding of how to outsmart your spaniel, or in some cases your spouse.

We all want our pup to become Lassie—immediately. You know, the dog that walks casually on a loose leash with you to Starbucks and hangs out while you get your cup of java. Meanwhile, back in reality, your dog pulls you down the street to his own destination as you curse like a sailor, poop bag in hand.

When you first get your lovable Lab or Lhasa, you probably think, "How hard can this be? I can set a VCR. Raising a dog can't be brain surgery." Then all of a sudden, your new pup changes from Einstein to Jaws in a matter of weeks. Many people find they have a few bones to pick with their dog's behavior and discover they need to train their dog.

I wrote this book to help people deal with the normal stages of aggravating puppyhood. Even the well-versed dog owner may find some new treats here. Translating to dog owners, in a humorous way, how to unleash their pooch's potential within the framework of their daily routine is my main mission.

My very first dog, a poodle named Tiny Tim, gave whoever opened the front door a new workout ritual. At age five I thought that this was some weird exercise fad, a game where an adult answers the door and then chases a little black poodle down the street screaming his name. Even as a child I realized that Timmy was not a bad dog; he just didn't realize what everyone wanted from him. Tragically, Timmy was never trained and was hit by a car during one of his excursions. I was devastated.

I hounded my mom for another dog and I got my longtime wish—a German shepherd puppy—a twelfth-birthday present. I was old enough to take care of a dog by then, and determined to create an understanding that had been missing with Timmy. I weighed 60 pounds; my dog, Rex, grew to be 112 pounds. Oops! Wanting Rin Tin Tin, I sought out an obedience school, where I was the youngest student. After I had trained Rex to an enviable level of behavior in basic and advanced obedience, we graduated first in our class in off-leash obedience.

Since I seemed to have the knack, I decided to go on to work him in utility, agility, and confirmation training. Showing her support, my mom drove Rex and me to dog training class every Wednesday for two and half years. By the time I was fourteen years old, my neighbors were soliciting my advice in teaching their dogs, and a business was born.

The experience led me to study human psychology and mass communication at the University of Denver, where I earned my B.A. As I realized my Dr. Doolittle calling, I decided to combine my knowledge of human psychology with my insight into doggie delinquency. Shortly thereafter I settled in Los Angeles, training hundreds of people and their dogs along the way.

My business grew, with veterinarians referring clients to me. Word of mouth about my tail-wagging results led to the Hollywood homes of many celebrities, including Kevin Costner, Jim Carrey, and LeAnn Rimes, as well as studio executives, at-home moms, doctors, musicians, accountants, and electricians, among others. The real scoop about celebrity dog owners is that they have the same concerns about their pampered pooches as we all do about our own pups.

In 1997, I was honored in *Los Angeles* magazine by being named the best dog trainer in L.A. I also produced and hosted a weekly call-in radio show, where I let out the truth about canines and their companions. Teaching people positive patterns with their pups gave the pet industry a juicy bone to chew.

Canine behaviorial problems are my specialty. I solve cases involving dog aggression, territorialism, fear biting, spot peeing, separation anxiety, destructive chewing, excessive barking, and other neurotic responses. Surprisingly, many of the dogs I deal with have often had some form of obedience training. I find that the problem is not the dog itself but the owner, who hasn't been shown how and where to apply training within his or her routine. And although we may all be close to perfect, some of our endearing personality quirks can confuse our pups, not to mention other family members.

It should always be remembered that to have a happy relationship the needs of both the dog and the dog owner must be met. The key to training is to keep it simple and fun. All dogs want to please. You just need to know the clearest, most consistent way to guide them. So if you feel doggedly challenged raising your new best friend, keep reading. Whether you are a celebrity who travels a lot, a mother of three juggling a tight schedule, or a single professional working ten hours a day, you can do it. You can have the hangin' hound.

The Dating Game

A dog is the only thing on this earth
that loves you more than he loves
himself.
—JOSH BILLINGS

We are all conditioned to want the perfect dog. I call this the Lassie syndrome. Whether you are drawn to a sporty spaniel or a sophisticated Saluki, what you need to realize is that a puppy is a puppy. It doesn't matter whether you are still dating, or in puppy love, or discovering doggy delinquency, it's never too late to read this book. Know that you *can* teach an old dog new tricks. If you've brought home a puppy and your first thought is, "Oh no, what did I do?" or "How much can this little dog poop?" well, don't panic. Let's find out whether you have met your match.

Are you picking out a puppy or do you already have one? Getting a dog is sort of like dating. What you see is not always what you're going to get. Reaching the level of happy muttrimony takes effort, time, and a sense of humor.

Like dating, finding the right canine match requires having a good understanding of your own likes, dislikes, and habits, as well as finding the right chemistry. Chemistry depends on the temperament of the dog and how well it fits into your individual circumstances. In deciding on the right temperament, find out whether you are attracted to a diva or a shaggy shy guy, a pup who barks back or one who rolls over. The "Animal Attraction" section in this chapter will alert you to the many mutt-matching possibilities.

It doesn't really matter whether you fall in love with a pure-bred or a mongrel, as long as you're ready for the commitment. You wouldn't spend the next fifteen years of your life with just anyone. So before you begin to train your pooch it is helpful to know if you have found your match. Knowing whether you have a compatible companion will give you insight into whether raising your dog will be an uphill struggle or a ride down easy street. This chapter will highlight the most important factors in choosing the right pooch partner for your lifestyle.

All relationships take time to develop, and raising a dog is no different. We can't pick our relatives, but we can create a great relationship with our new best friend. Understanding what type of person you are is half the battle in finding the right canine companion. Are you a triathlete or a couch potato? Do you live uptown or downtown? Are you a control freak or is everything just plain O.K. with you? Assessing your lifestyle is important in both choosing a dog and successfully reaching Lassie level without major damage.

ENERGY LEVEL

A main factor to consider when choosing a breed is your own energy level. Are you a low- or high-maintenance person? A good exercise for choosing the right dog for your lifestyle is to write down qualities that would best describe your own personality. As crazy as that sounds, the list will give you a general idea of what kind of temperament and energy level you should look for in a breed of dog.

Many behavioral issues stem from a dog's needs not being met properly. Exercise is the number one factor. Just like people, certain breeds are more high-strung and need more exercise than others. Still, every dog needs to be walked daily and all young dogs need a great deal of exercise well into adulthood.

Believe it or not, the energy level of the breed you choose matters a great deal in training. If you are a mellow person who mistakenly chooses a dog based on looks alone and then finds that his energy level exceeds your basic needs, you could have to cope with an unfortunate mismatch. The following list was established mainly to create awareness. Here are some of the more popular breeds that fit into either the high- or the low-maintenence category.

• *Good low-maintenance companions,* in terms of exercise, are breeds such as Bulldogs and toy and miniature breeds, like Yorkshire Terriers, West Highland Terriers, Cocker Spaniels, and Poodles, to name a few. A walk around the block, along with play time, will suffice. Other low-maintenance dogs are the very large breeds, like Saint Bernards, Great Danes, and Great Pyrenees. However, these dogs will still be quite active during puppyhood, since all young dogs are rambunctious and need daily exercise and stimulation.

• *High-maintenance companions,* in terms of exercise, are breeds like Jack Russells, Dalmatians, Rottweilers, Dobermans, German Shepherds, Golden Retrievers, Labradors, Pointers, Standard Poodles, Terriers, and most herding breeds. I call these types ball-aholics. So warm up your throwing arm and put on running shoes if you live in an apartment with any of these dogs.

Again, there are always exceptions to the rule in terms of individual temperaments within each breed. Also, dogs over the age of four years tend to become lower maintenance. After all, age mellows all of us. Don't forget, you can adopt an adult dog that needs a good home at a shelter or breed rescue facility.

 PAW PRINT: Fossil records suggest that the dog was domesticated 14,000 years ago.

WHERE YOU LIVE

Thank goodness, dogs couldn't care less about whether we live uptown or downtown? That's one of the things that make them so great. But where you live can influence how difficult it may be to raise your pup. It is important to be realistic about your circumstances. Is your neighborhood a safe place to walk at night? Do you like to be outdoors? To spend time in parks? Do you travel frequently or not at all?

Location, location, location can be a major factor in how convenient it will be for you to have a dog. Sure, we all would like the big house with a backyard, but it isn't always possible. Big dog, small apartment: Is it a good idea? Many people pick a pocket-size pooch because they live in a small place or travel often. Singer LeAnn Rimes adores her portable Pomeranian, Raven. Its small size is a definite plus because LeAnn likes to take Raven along on the road when she tours. Toy breeds do not need as much space as a collie, but don't forget, they still need exercise and to go outside to the bathroom four to five times a day, regardless of the weather.

Renting with Rover

Owning a dog and living in an apartment can be difficult. Believe me, I have done it. If you work at home, it becomes easier. However, most of us are away at a job eight or ten hours a day, and finding the time to housebreak, train, and exercise the dog on a daily basis can be challenging. The main bone of contention for apartment-dwelling dog parents is housebreaking. You will get all the juicy details on how to accomplish this as you read on. (See Chapter 6 in particular.)

When you live in an apartment, your dog's age matters. A puppy becomes calmer as he matures, but be prepared for some trying times during the first year of development. You may worry that the neighbors are going to complain about some barking. There will be *many* elevator rides to take the pup out. But if you're still game, dog walkers can be a relatively inexpensive way to help you through the housebreaking stage. (See Chapter 12, "At Your Service.")

"No Pets Allowed"— What to Do?

Even if your dream apartment does not allow pets, there may be a way to get around it. Begin by creating a résumé for your dog. Sound stupid? It worked for me.

I once lived in a one-bedroom apartment, in a building where pets were not allowed, with not one but two German Shepherds. The following tips are for pet owners facing a similar predicament.

• Do not ask prospective landlords if the building allows pets. Go see if you like the place first. Also, check to make sure it is close to a park.

• Compose your dog's résumé. Be sure to include:

  1. Your dog's name, age, and breed.
  2. A letter from a former landlord or neighbor attesting to your dog's good behavior. Ask the writer to include a phone number, too.
  3. A letter from your vet, describing your dog's health and the flea control products that are used.
  4. A dog training certificate from a group obedience class or a letter from a trainer, stating that your dog has completed basic obedience and has no housebreaking problems or separation anxiety.
  5. A picture of your pup.

• Meet the prospective landlord without your dog. If you like the landlord and feel you can approach the issue, give him or her the résumé and ask if the rules can be bent.

If you don't like the landlord, then the potential problems with neighbors or building managers simply are not worth it. Look elsewhere. However, if you make the effort and people see that you are conscientious, then most of the time a nice, dog-friendly landlord will give you a chance.

Homeowners

Good for you, you have a backyard. The danger here is thinking that you're home free in the housebreaking department. WRONG. The number one mistake homeowners make is to leave their puppy outside all day, thinking they will save themselves a cleanup.

Do not leave your pup in the yard all day. The youngster will go to the bathroom whenever he feels the urge. Although this might seem to be the easiest solution, you need to formally teach the dog how to hold it. Avoiding such training will only create housebreaking issues later.

Similarly, people often feel that their puppy can exercise itself in a yard. They neglect to spend time playing with him. Behavioral problems like excessive digging and barking (due to boredom and a lack of socialization) can stem from not exercising your puppy.

Having a backyard does not exclude you from walking duties, either. Going for a walk is one of a dog's greatest pleasures and it is your responsibility to give him the opportunity to learn about his surroundings. There are hundreds of interesting things for him to smell and see on each walk. A good walk also helps your dog to be more relaxed later inside the house.

GREAT EXPECTATIONS

Dogs have become the ultimate accessory. Many people choose a cute puppy or dog without doing enough research on the breed, background, and temperament of the dog. They just like the way it looks.

Too many people choose a dog based on false notions. Notions that one breed of dog is easier to train than another, or is better with children, are not always true. It's like saying blondes are bubble-heads or bankers are boring. Stereotypes can prove to be false in the dog world, just as they are among humans. Labrador Retrievers make good hunting dogs, but some are bred to lead the blind. Of course, not all breeds have such versatility. For instance, I would have a hard time visualizing a Basset Hound leading the blind.

Years ago I got a call from a troubled couple, John and Melanie, who had held off getting a puppy until their second daughter was two years old. Finally, John got his dream dog—a purebred Labrador named Rascal. John had researched different dog breeders and found one of the finest local kennels with high-quality Labs, where he got his pup. Yet his first words to me were "Help! This puppy is like the Energizer rabbit on speed! He will not stop jumping and biting. He won't settle down."

When I visited the family I discovered a great couple with two little girls, both under the age of six, and a three-and-a-half-month-old, very dominant male pup. This was a well-bred pup from a long line of Labrador Retrievers that had excelled as duck hunters. Rascal was alert and eager, with built-in endurance to run through fields and the temperament to remain unfazed by the sound of rifle shots. In short, a swell dog if you lived in the country and competed in field and trial events, but not for a city family busy raising young children.

I recommended that they reexamine this match. John was a successful television executive with little free time. I asked him if he wanted to take up duck hunting as a hobby. He smiled, with a look as if to say "Not in this lifetime." Melanie's priority as a busy mom was attending to her two small girls.

Both John and Melanie wanted a family dog, though. They asked if Rascal could be trained. I explained that their puppy's needs far exceeded what their lifestyle could supply. They thought that as a trainer I would drill the pup and change his ways. And in most cases, I would teach the owner and the pup how to get through doggie delinquency.

But to their surprise, I described an alternative solution. As a behaviorist, I had to consider what was best for the dog as well as the family. "What if I got you a three-year-old, nonteething, loving dog who won't knock your children down?" I asked. Melanie's eyes lit up like a green traffic light.

Rascal was still young enough (under four months old) to be placed in another home by his original breeder. In fact, there was a waiting list for such sporting dogs. Rascal was quickly placed with a family in the country, where his energy was valued for hunting and ranching.

After looking through dog rescue facilities for a few weeks, I came across a three-year-old, spayed female Golden Retriever mix named Molly, who had been raised with children. She had an easy nature, but she was up for adoption because the family had one too many dogs. John, Melanie, and the children met Molly and it was a love match. With a little training, the family got their perfect pooch. John wound down after work by throwing the ball to his favorite outfielder, Melanie got a great walking companion, and the girls enjoyed a cuddly playmate.

The moral of this story is do your research, not solely on the breed of dog but also the range of temperament within the breed. And always keep in mind the realities of your own lifestyle.

Animal Attraction

Picking the pup with the right temperament to match your own is the key to achieving the hangin' hound. How do you choose? If there were mutt-matching personals, an ad might read: "Normal person seeks nice dog. Preferably one that doesn't bark back." Finding a match isn't so easy. Just as there will be a variety of temperaments among the children in any family, the same goes for any litter within a breed. I have identified seven different typical temperaments. Decide which type of doggie personality suits you best.

- *Shy Guy.* This pup will carry his tail down and hesitate to run toward you at first sight. But once you crouch down and clap your hands, he will run to you with obvious affection. A pup like this will need guidance from you and will need to be taught positive boundaries because he may be very needy in general. *Training will boost his confidence and security.* He will need to be socialized, but with the right parent he could be a perfect companion and great family dog.

- *The Diva.* She has an independent and aloof nature. This Greta Garbo type would prefer to be left alone. She stands out easily because she separates herself from the pack. To test, if you walk away from her in a room, she may not follow. *One-on-one training and bonding are musts.* With training, this cool cucumber will show her sweet side. When mature, the temperamental temptress is a perfect apartment pet and cat companion. Great for the at-home, workaholic dog parent because a quick walk around the block will suffice for her. One prerequisite is space: the diva does not like to be crowded. Homes with large families are not her style.

- *The Flirty Girl.* This tail-wagging party girl definitely needs a backyard for prancing. She is a family girl, great with children and other dogs. This wild child will jump up on you and your couch with gusto. It doesn't mean she's not intelligent, it's just that she has too many places to go and too many people to see. To have this flighty female stuck in an apartment all day would be a drag. Without a proper workout on a daily basis, she will probably get into trouble. *Dog parks and group training classes are her idea of a good time.* She generally loves to chase things, so watch out for the neighbor's cat.

• *Mr. Macho Man.* Contrary to popular belief, this testosterone-totin' pooch comes in all sizes, Chihuahua to Rottweiler. You will know him when you meet him. He will make no bones about coming up to you and marking his territory with powerful kisses. This pup is not an armchair athlete. He is energetic and must not only watch a game but be a player. If he is not guided in the right direction early, all of his ambitious drive will go into doggy delinquency. *With attention, training, and love, this pooch can and should go all the way to Harvard (advanced obedience).* He would be too rambunctious to raise for parents with children under the age of ten.

• *The Big Lug.* He is not the sharpest tool in the shed. But this friendly fellow can be a loving companion. The only problem is that he comes in only one size: big. You will not find this temperament among toy or medium-size breeds. So if you don't like dog hair or lots of dog slobber, this guy is not for you. He is a great family choice, but you need to have the room for him. You will find this gentle giant sleeping under anything he can fit beneath. His favorite pastimes are eating and sleeping, with short spurts of energy in between. *Training will help keep his mind alert and give him love in return.* Keep in mind that large-boned puppies have a lot of growing to do and can be prone to health problems if they were not not bred properly; so do your research.

• *The Wallflower.* This precious pup comes in all sizes and shapes and both sexes. Like some people, some dogs are just shy. A puppy with his tail tucked under at all times is not innately trusting. This temperament can be alluring if you are a nurturing caregiver, but there are some dangers. Many owners drawn to the subordinate type of pup tend to be overly protective and coddle this nervous Nelly, adding to behavioral problems. *Training this pup is the only way to bring out the confidence it needs to have a good life.* The Wallflower would be a terrible match for a person who has an extroverted lifestyle, or a loud household with children. However, if you are a single dog owner with patience and time, this could be your baby.

Whichever temperament appeals to you, keep in mind that all puppies need to be trained. Some dogs will learn eagerly, others will be easily distracted, but any dog's ultimate success will depend on *your* ability to teach him consistently, not with discipline but in a positive, pleasant way. Blaming it on the dog won't work anymore. So make sure you have a good assessment of your own energy level and environment before making your choice. Keep reading and find out whether you are attracted to a pound pooch or a pedigreed pup.

POUND POOCH OR PEDIGREED PUP?

Picking a pound pooch or a pedigreed pup is simply a personal choice. I own one of each. For your search, I recommend going to a city dog shelter as well as a few private breeders. This way you can get a true assessment of where your heart belongs.

A good way to guess the potential adult size of a pup is to weigh the dog at the age of four months and then double that number. You can estimate a dog's age by its teeth. Baby teeth fall out and adult choppers are in place by the age of six months. At three years of age, there is usually an amount of tartar build-up on the back molars. But don't try prying open every hound's mouth for a full exam. A quick look will do.

Pound and Rescued Pups

You can find city dog shelters listed in your local phone book, or through a veterinarian's office. Sometimes pet supply stores carry free magazines that advertise many great dogs that need homes. Looking for a Labrador or Lhasa Apso? Don't forget to check breed rescue groups, which are listed with vets, groomers, and pet supply stores. Rescue organizations save unwanted dogs and puppies and care for them until they are placed in loving homes.

When rescuing Rover, ask the shelter or rescue personnel to give you any background information they may have on him. Ask to see the dog in a holding area, so you can get acquainted. City shelters have a wide range of dogs, from young pups to adults of every size and breed. New dogs arrive on a daily basis. Unfortunately, after a limited amount of time, dogs that are not placed are killed. Breed rescue groups keep pets until they are adopted. Remember, with a little training even an old dog can learn new tricks, so don't feel limited to adopting a puppy.

You should not assume that a dog is trained, or housebroken, just because it's not a puppy. You will have to train any dog to know the rules of your home.

Pamper your pooch by getting all the bowls, balls, teething toys, and food before bringing him home. (See Chapter 3, "All the Things You Need and Nothing More.")

Pedigreed Pups

There are three types of dog breeders: professional, private, and backyard. I recommend interviewing a number of breeders and looking at several litters before making a choice. With each type of breeder there are certain things to keep in mind as you search. Buying a puppy from a pet store instead of directly from a breeder is not advisable.

Professional Breeders

These people are in the dog business, literally. You'll find them on the Internet, listed according to breed, or you can check with the American Kennel Club. Many own large kennel facilities that breed dogs for show. What this means is that they are in a race to meet the requirements of a breed standard, and so the physical attributes of a specific breed rule.

Granted that the temperament of the dog is considered in the breeding game, but champion qualities are regarded mainly in terms of beauty, beefcake, and bearing. Just because a dog comes from champion lineage does not mean that its overall health and temperament are guaranteed.

Professional breeders often keep the pick of their litters and sell puppies they deem "pet quality." This isn't necessarily bad, but you should know what you are buying and not be overly impressed with a dog's blue-blooded background. These pups can be pricey—$800 and up.

A good professional breeder will answer any questions you have about the health, temperament, and background of a dog. He or she should also be able to explain linebreeding and cross-breeding.

If you are offered a co-ownership contract, be careful. This contract generally requires you to raise the dog, while giving the breeder a right to show it and possibly breed it in the future. I do not recommend this arrangement. It is best to own your puppy outright.

If show dogs are your bag of bones, then by all means look in your local newspaper for dog show events and breed specialty matches or call the AKC and get in the game.

Private Breeders

These breeders offer one or two litters a year, or every other year. Although they may consider their service a hobby, many private breeders do know a great deal about dogs. They breed mainly for temperament. Private breeders are listed in the classified section of your local newspaper under Pets. If you are searching for a reasonably priced pet, this is the way to go.

Make sure that you like the breeder and that the breeder is able to show you either one or both of the puppy's parents. A responsible breeder will not breed an immature female that is still a puppy herself. It is best if the mother of the puppies is at least two years old and has a good temperament. The puppies should be raised in a clean environment, in a home rather than a kennel.

Ask the breeder why he decided to have his dog bred and how he chose the sire of the pups. Both parents should have AKC pedigree certificates. The breeder should be able to explain the papers to you. A good breeder will interview you as well, and assist you in selecting a puppy that will suit your lifestyle.

Backyard Breeders

Be careful. You will find these breeders in the newspaper as well. You will have to use your own judgment as to whether the person sounds decent. Usually a backyard breeder will not want to have a lengthy phone conversation with you. Instead he or she will try to convince you to come look at the pups, hoping that once there you will fall in love and just go ahead and buy a puppy. Often such breeders will not be able to produce the proper AKC pedigree papers because they do not breed dogs selectively. If you cannot meet the mother of the puppies, walk away. It is a dead giveaway of bad news. The mother is key to gauging the quality of the dog and its inherited temperament. This type of breeder will probably not ask you any questions about your living conditions or lifestyle. Primarily, he or she only wants to sell the dog.

Pet Stores
No reputable breeder sells puppies to pet stores. Pet stores generally buy from puppy mills at a low cost and then sell the pups for at least double the price. Not only can it be more costly to buy from a store than from a breeder, but the dog's heritage is unknown. I always want to rescue these poor pups from the store, but I know that buying a dog from the pet store encourages this awful business. Since puppy mill dogs are usually bred under bad conditions, genetically these pups can be a mess, and you could find out later with much heartache and massive vet bills. Not recommended.

HEALTH CHECK

Other than its having a cold nose, how do you know if a pup is healthy? Just because a purebred pup comes from championship lineage does not mean it is healthy. Equally, every pooch from the pound does not always carry an illness. It really boils down to the luck of the draw.

The following are a few of the more common genetic health concerns that should be addressed with breeders before you purchase a pup.

In pedigreed pups, each breed can be prone to specific ailments. Ask the breeder about any known skin allergies or hip problems common to the breed of dog that interests you. In toy and small breeds, underbites and overbites of the jaw can be a sign of bad breeding and are problematic.

Popular breeds like Labs, German Shepherds, Golden Retrievers, and Bernese Mountain Dogs, among others, are prone to hip dysplasia—where the hip joints of the dog do not fit properly in the hip sockets and loose ligaments do not hold the hip in place. This is a moderately heritable condition, which can lead to progressive structural changes over time. Even dogs with normal hips can produce dysplastic pups. Some of the early signs of hip dysplasia are pain in the hip, difficulty in getting up, and a swaying gait or bunny hops when running.

Most reputable breeders will be open to discussing health issues. Ask to see the pedigree certificate and look for the letters OFA. They stand for Orthopedic Foundation for Animals. Responsible breeders of large dogs have their dogs X-rayed and are assigned an OFA number to show certification before they breed them.

Although information about a dog's background may be limited at a shelter, the staff members who feed the dogs should be able to give you their assessment of a pup's health and temperament. Puppies and dogs are always medically assessed and inoculated when they enter a city shelter, and shelters usually have an on-staff vet. Ask the vet about possible signs of mange or skin allergies and about the general health of any dog you are considering. Shelters require you to pay for spaying or neutering before releasing a dog to you. Always take a pound pup to your vet for an overall checkup within the first few days of adopting it.

Obvious Signs of an Unhealthy Pup

- Listlessness
- Dull coat
- Hair loss
- Constant scratching
- Runny eyes or nose
- Hop or swing in the back end when running
- Limping
- Distended stomach, tucked tail, or extreme weight loss

ALLERGIC TO YOUR OWN BEST FRIEND?

Are you or a family member allergic to dogs? A frequent question for people choosing a dog is, "Which breeds are best for people with allergies?"

A number of myths surround the subject of dogs and allergies. Most people think that it is the dog's fur, or shedding alone, that causes allergic reactions. In fact, it is not so much shedding that causes a reaction, it's something called dander.

Dander comes from the dog's skin. As the dog licks itself, the skin becomes dry and flakes off. Those flakes are called dander. Dogs that are prone to skin problems create a lot of dander which, when airborne, can make allergies act up.

According to many allergy specialists, there are no "allergy-free" dogs. All dogs carry dander, whether they shed or not. There are a few exotic breeds that are actually hairless, but this does not exempt them from skin conditions.

So you're thinking, "Great, my only choice is getting a rare breed that has no hair!" Well, there is hope for the people who are allergic to dogs. There are more new products on the market every year that can help. One of these is Allerpet, a solution to spray on your pet's fur to help control dander.

Some likely low-allergy breed candidates are Poodles and Bichon Frises. Poodles shed very little and come in three different sizes—toy, miniature, and standard. Each is bred in seven different colors: blue, black, silver, brown, white, apricot, and cream. (Poodles get a bad rap due to their odd haircuts, as seen in dog shows. They can look like adorable little lambs with the right groomer.) The Bichon Frise, a small white fluffy breed weighing seven to twelve pounds, also has minimal shedding. In addition, I know people with allergies who have lived happily with Tibetan Terriers and a few other breeds. However, because of the individual nature of allergies, do your own research.

Please try to visit several breeders or shelters and spend time with the type of dog you are interested in. See how you react before accepting the responsibility of a new pup. For people who are highly allergic to dogs, I recommend bathing your dog every other week, which may help control dander. Make sure that you rinse your dog well because residual shampoo left on the dog can cause scratching and dry out the skin.

Stay away from breeds that are traditionally prone to skin problems—Cocker Spaniels, Dalmatians, Sharpeis and many others. Breeds that shed a lot include Golden Retrievers, German Shepherds, and Labrador Retrievers, even though Labs have a short coat.

LOOKING FOR LASSIE

I own a German Shepherd named Bo who is definitely Mr. Macho Man in temperament. As a trainer, I was up for the challenge. Bo originally came from a private breeder, but I actually rescued him in a way. A man had called me for training, and when I showed up he handed me an Arnold Schwarzenegger–like, three-month-old German Shepherd puppy and told me to keep it.

The puppy was purchased as a gift for a man who lived in a condo, owned his own company, and worked ten-hour days. He simply could not be a father to an active puppy (well, a brute, to be more accurate). I was stunned, and sort of excited. I have owned German Shepherds all of my life, so I could not say no.

I told myself it was best to take the pup so that I could find him a good home. And that was that. I was the mother of a very large baby boy with enormous ears. Bo and I were a match. His dominant personality led him to be the best demonstration dog I have ever had. Bo loves car rides and meeting my clients and showing off his education.

Three years after I got Bo, I ran into a flirty girl who worked the room like Madonna. I rescued my second dog, Miss Daisy, from a local shelter. I had been asked to make an appearance on a morning TV show and to pick two puppies to give away on the air. I went to a local shelter and was blown away by the number of dogs that people had discarded.

It was difficult to choose, but I was mainly looking for two dogs, average size, with exceptional temperament and in good health. As I walked through the kennel, I saw a group of four medium-size dogs sleeping amid the loud barking. I stopped and whistled, which woke up all of them. One dog backed away out of fear, two started barking, and then there was Daisy, just wagging her tail like a neon sign. A five-month-old terrier mix, medium size, not too dominant and not too submissive.

I chose her and another puppy for the show. Daisy ended up getting sick a couple of days before the show and was not able to go to the television station. The day after the show, I called the shelter, asking about her condition. They said she was much better but would be put to sleep that day, since her time at the shelter had elapsed. I was horrified, canceled my appointments, and went to get her. Once again, my intention was to find her a home with one of my clients. The rest is history, as they say.

Daisy proved to be a perfect addition to my family. Although I was not looking for another dog of my own, I did go to the shelter with specific requirements in mind for a good pet. Fortunately, at that point in my life I had the time to integrate a second dog into my household.

 PAW PRINT The world's oldest dog, an Australian cattle dog, lived to be 29 years old.

Matching Fidos with Their Famous Masters

Do you think an individual's personality plays a big part in the type of dog he or she chooses? You guessed right. See if you have anything in common with some of our favorite celebrities. Try to match them with their canine companions. Match a celebrity (number) with the breed (letter) you think he or she owns and see how well you do.

1. Kevin Costner
2. Jason Priestley
3. Ricky Martin
4. LeAnn Rimes
5. Oprah Winfrey
6. Peter Norton
7. Will Smith
8. Alicia Silverstone
9. Bette Midler
10. Elizabeth Taylor

a. Pomeranian
b. Maltese
c. Standard Poodle
d. French Bulldog
e. Jack Russell Terrier
f. Labrador Retrievers
g. Golden Retriever, Chihuahua
h. Cocker Spaniels, Golden Retrievers
i. Many mixed-breeds
j. Rottweilers

ANSWERS: 1f, 2d, 3g, 4a, 5h, 6c, 7j, 8i, 9e, 10b

PAW PRINT The first official dog show in the United States took place in 1859.

Five Tips to Happy Muttrimony

1.   The commitment of owning a pet for ten to fifteen years is a serious one. Have as many doggie dates as possible. Interview different breeders. Visit animal shelters and see lots of pups to get a good sense of their temperament before saying "I do."

2.   One breed of dog is not necessarily easier to raise than another. Within any particular breed of dog there is a spectrum of different temperaments.

3.   Choosing the right breed and temperament for your lifestyle means being honest with yourself about the amount of time and energy you are willing to commit to raising a dog.

4.   Consider the age of the dog. Don't rule out an older dog because it may not be as "cute" as a puppy. With age comes wisdom, even in dogs, and the calmer nature of an adult dog might be perfect for you.

5.   It's best to assume that your dog knows nothing and train him from scratch to suit your lifestyle.

 PAW PRINT: What breed originated in Tibet thousands of years ago and is thought to have fought lions, tigers, and bears? Answer: the Mastiff.

For better or for worse, in sickness and in health . . . Congratulations, you've made your choice. You're a dog owner. In the next chapter, "The Seven Breeds of Dog Owners," you'll see that choosing a breed may have a double meaning. I have created a humorous way for people to recognize their own quirks and understand how their behavior affects their dogs. So if you find yourself doggedly challenged, keep reading.

CHAPTER

2

The Seven Breeds of Dog Owners

Laughter is like the human body
wagging its tail.
—ANNE WILSON SCHAEF

Most people are surprised, then laugh with an affirming roll of the eyes, when they realize that *they* are my primary students, not their dogs. You're probably thinking, "Why should I read about my own temperament in a dog training book?" Well, "The Seven Breeds of Dog Owners" is based on human behavior patterns that affect canine performance. It gives us a way to see how our actions shape our dog's behavior.

All humans have habits and special quirks that will inevitably impact their dogs. We just don't always see them—unless someone is kind enough to point them out to us. For instance, some of us have lengthy conversations with our dogs, attempting to teach them commands. Others try coaxing, whining, or even begging. This can be embarrassing and can actually contribute to, or in some cases create, misbehavior in your dog.

Different dog-owner personalities—or breeds, as I call them—can surface during different stages of your dog's development. So don't be surprised if you start out by identifying with the Coaxer and end up relating most to the Control Freak by the time your puppy is eight months old.

A common bone of contention can be discussing Sparky with your spouse. I have been in many homes where couples get a dog and one of the two (and I won't mention the gender) has his or her own theory of puppy raising that would make even your dog's tail curl. Winging it can create a pile of problems. One partner may be in dog-owner denial or an absolute tyrant when it comes to puppy training. To some, an obedient dog means discipline, while other partners are anarchists at heart. This kind of philosophical opposition could give a dog whiplash. Although we may find our own inconsistencies endearing, for dogs they are just plain confusing.

Recognizing your own traits and those of your partner and other family members helps undo some human habits that get in the way of successfully teaching your dog. This awareness will help you see your role in the process of training your pooch. My *people-training* approach is important to understand before getting to the mechanics of obedience. Consistency and positive reinforcement together are the trick to make your dream dog happen.

The key, in any relationship, is to know thyself.

Dogs follow patterns and become consistently inconsistent to our inconsistencies. Are you confused? Just think how your dog feels.

The ability to recognize yourself in the process of training your dog will help you check your own behavior before you start to influence your dog negatively. Your dog will thank you, your friends will thank you, and maybe even a relative or two will thank you as well. No matter our age, occupation, or disposition, we all fit one or more of the seven personality types. Just remember that behaviors take time to develop in people—and this is true with dogs, too.

 PAW PRINT: There are 400 dog breeds worldwide.

More often than not, it's our behavior that creates automatic misbehaviors in our dog.

Which of the following dog-owner breeds sounds like you? And does any of the seven breeds describe a family member?

BREED #1: THE COAXER

Do you feel if you repeat a command often enough, sooner or later your dog will catch on? Are your favorite words "Come on!"? Or do you call your dog's name a zillion times, hoping the dog will pay attention? If your actions fit this breed of dog owner, your dog is on his way to teaching *you* to beg!

Many puppy parents identify with this breed of dog owner. You may grow into a mixed breed in time, as your puppy matures. However, you need to understand how this common trait can affect your pup's perception.

Chew on this: If your dog could talk, his first word would be "WHAT?"

Identifying features: This person gets an A for effort, but is carrying the philosophy of repetition in dog training too far. The Coaxer comes in different shapes and sizes. Some Coaxer personalities insist their dog knows what they want him to do, but just won't do it. A fundamental problem arises from endless repeating of your dog's name without addressing what you want him to do. Actions prove louder than words.

The Coaxer breed of owner repeats the dog's name in order to get the dog's attention. This only teaches your dog to ignore you. As your dog matures, outside distractions, such as movement, smells, and sounds, will override your pleading voice inflection. Coaxing your dog can produce aloof behavior and mar the training process.

Bare-Bones Fact:
Don't beg or plead with your puppy. Learn how to guide him on a leash to please you.

BREED #2: THE CONTROL FREAK

Does the word "Hey" slip off your tongue when your dog bolts out the front door every time it opens? Do you find yourself yelling "Hey!" every time your dog jumps up on you?

This disciplinarian believes "Hey!" is a generic command to handle all situations. He or she generally owns the teenage pup.

Chew on this: As your dog is bolting out the front door, he's probably thinking, "Hey to you, too!"

Identifying features: This breed of dog owner misunderstands the concept of discipline and focuses primarily on negative reinforcement. The Control Freak often feels out of control because of his high expectations and extreme perfectionism. This approach attracts the wild child of the puppy world.

The following misbehaviors are possible consequences of the Control Freak's misguided form of reprimand: chewing furniture, grabbing food off the table, and jumping onto the couch, among other delinquencies.

This breed of dog owner has at least two or three meanings for "Hey!" He leaves it up to the dog to decipher what he means every time he shouts. Instead, the dog learns to tune him out and continue the behavior.

If you are laughing to yourself, or at yourself, it means you recognize that someone you know is a Control Freak mix, if not a purebred Control Freak. This breed of dog owner needs to learn to guide his dog in a positive way rather than allow unruly behavior to happen in the first place.

Does this sound familiar? "No, get down!" "Off!" "Hey! Stop it!" This was the chant of my client Jonathan Exley, celebrity photographer (*People, US, Rolling Stone, GQ*). Every time he returned home from a hectic day, his dog Lily, a Wheaten terrier mix, body-slammed him at the door. Albeit loving, this greeting annoyed Jonathan. "I need you to fix this, Inger," he said. "I love her madly, but Lily is being obnoxious."

Many people feel their dog behaves badly on purpose. A dog's exuberant hello is not necessarily a bad thing. However, if you want to change Fido's wild ways, the dog needs to be guided to please you.

The trouble is, we operate in large gray areas of thought. What we say is not always what we mean or want. Dogs have clarity. They do not think, "I sort of feel like chasing that squirrel, but maybe I should listen to my owner." The squirrel runs, the dog chases it. Jonathan's problem could be solved by kindly directing his dog to "Sit." The chant "No, get down!" "Off!" "Hey! Stop it!" regardless of how loud, did not tell Lily what she *should* do. A pleasant command is worth a thousand reprimands.

Bare-Bones Fact:
Your dog's training is only as good as the way you
apply it.

BREED #3: THE SMACKER

Do you roll up a newspaper and smack your dog on the nose when he does something wrong? Do you feel sparing the rod is spoiling the spaniel?

<u>*Chew on this:*</u> You should NEVER, EVER HIT YOUR DOG.

O.K., I know many owners do not perceive themselves as abusive or violent people. Somewhere along the road, they heard that when a dog has done something wrong, a light bop on the dog's nose will teach it not to misbehave. Wrong. Under no circumstance should you ever hit your dog.

Hitting your dog does not serve any purpose. We pat our dogs with our hand and use hand signals for advanced obedience. If you use the same hand to hit your dog (even when holding a rolled-up newspaper), you are sending a mixed signal. Teaching a dog to be obedient should be achieved through positive reinforcement, not punishment. Aggression can lead to aggression.

The Smacker breed of dog owner needs to get a better handle on understanding the dog's developmental stages, rather than trying to dominate the dog. Lead your dog, praise him. Don't terrorize him!

<u>*Identifying features:*</u> The Smacker's philosophy allows a dog's misbehavior to happen in the first place, because this owner is incorrectly disciplining a behavior that has already happened. All dogs

want to please; they just don't know how, until you take the time to show them. Remember that achieving your vision of Lassie does not happen overnight, and often a puppy's speed of retention is limited by its developmental stage. For example, a four-month-old puppy does not know *not* to chew on your hand or furniture; it is teething. All of its teeth need to come loose and fall out so new adult teeth can grow in.

The Smacker may feel the need to control this developmental stage by hitting the dog or reprimanding him for such natural behavior as teething. This can cause misbehavior from dogs, such as spot peeing out of fear. The dog may also learn to dodge his owner as a reaction to strong, improper reprimands, or even try to bite.

Bare-Bones Fact:
Obedience is the result of positive reinforcement, not discipline.

BREED #4: THE OL' EVIL EYE

Do you have special eye signals or gestures that you think your dog understands when you disapprove of something? Do you find your dog speaks more than you do? Are you training your dog through osmosis or ESP?

This owner tries to communicate through facial expressions and grunts, rather than clear commands and positive voice inflection. Ol' Evil Eye righteously feels his dog knows what it has done wrong when he gives his pooch the Ol' Evil Eye glare.

Chew on this: Your dog may be thinking many things, but your dog is not thinking of ways to correct his own behavior.

Identifying features: It seems to be Murphy's Law that this breed of dog owner always attracts, or ends up choosing, a submissive dog rather than a dominant one. The dominant dog would be able to handle such eye contact, creating a different set of issues. Due to this owner's lack of voice inflection, positive reinforcement, or use of boundaries, the dog never really knows where it stands or whether it's being good or bad.

Various dog behaviors can manifest themselves as a reaction to

Ol' Evil Eye's peculiarities. In cases of extreme misunderstanding, this owner's behavior can exacerbate spot peeing in an already submissive dog. Spot peeing is a neurotic response where the dog urinates uncontrollably as a reaction to its owner's overbearing exactitude.

This act of urinating or spot peeing occurs not because the dog does not know how to go to the bathroom outside, but it is born out of anxiety on the dog's part about how to please its owner. Hence, spot peeing is a form of behavioral incontinence. If this aplies to your dog, then see Chapter 11, "Working out the Kinks," to correct the problem.

Another common symptom due to lack of communication is the dog's complete inattention to its owner. We have all witnessed this type of interaction at one time or another—the high-spirited dog who completely ignores his owner's silent attempt to settle him down. The Ol' Evil Eye's minimalist approach unintentionally causes disobedience and creates confusion for the dog. This breed of owner needs to remember that a little communication and lots of positive reinforcement when the dog is on the leash goes a long way.

Bare-Bones Fact:
Actions speak louder than looks.

BREED #5: THE WHINER

Do you sound the same whether you are happy or sad? Do you think your dog is brilliant because he constantly cocks his head? The Whiner says "No" and "Good Dog" all in the same tone of voice. The problem with this breed of dog owner is that the dog must become a linguist in order to understand whether the owner is pleased or not.

**Chew on this:** "No!" should differ from other words in its tonality; it should be spoken using a low, quick, and firm inflection.

**Identifying features:** This owner thinks their dog is brilliant, mainly because the dog is constantly cocking its head, trying to understand them. As a trainer, I encounter this breed of dog owner often. What such owners need to know is that dogs respond to high-pitched sounds, which is why their dog cocks its head when they speak. I assure you, the dog is not trying to correct the owner's grammar.

One symptom of this breed of dog owner is that his or her voice inflection never varies. If the word "No" is said in a sweet, whiny voice, it will never set a boundary for the pup. Most new dog parents are members of this breed, especially when they first bring their puppy home. Although he or she may grow into a completely different breed of dog owner later, the Whiner says positive and negative things all in the same tone. This gives the dog a mixed signal. Usually the owner's tone of voice is nice enough, yet unfortunately the dog can't distinguish where its boundaries are.

Bare-Bones Fact:
Your dog does not understand English, French, or
Spanish, so don't attempt to explain things ad nauseam.
Match your tone to the message you want to convey
when training your dog.

BREED #6: THE "IT'S O.K." OWNER

For this breed of dog owner absolutely anything goes. Your dog poops on the floor every other week for a lifetime, and you will simply clean it up. While resenting this role, the owner generally feels that life has dealt him a bad hand and that there is nothing he can do to correct his dog's behavior.

Chew on this: While you are waiting for your dog to signal when he needs to go to the bathroom, he is wondering, "Why in the world don't you take me outside regularly?"

Identifying features: The symptom this dog owner's behavior creates is that the dog has the "occasional accident"—for a lifetime. We have all been to that house where there are too many potted plants in the living room, covering all the stains on the carpet from the dog. For a mature dog, urinating in the house is due to a lack of boundaries and therefore becomes an act of dominance, not just a matter of housebreaking. This behavior could be corrected by crating and training the dog in different areas of the house, but not by this passive parent. This breed of dog owner generally owns a small or toy breed of dog.

Bare-Bones Fact:
Training should be incorporated into your daily routine.

BREED #7: THE TALKER

Do you give your dog a dissertation on your daily activities? Do you wonder if your dog is stupid or just plain stubborn when he doesn't listen? The Talker breed of owner would probably be genuinely surprised to know that dogs, though quite perceptive, simply don't understand lengthy human conversation.

Chew on this: Dogs do not reason. If they did, you could have them pick up your dry cleaning or balance your checkbook.

Identifying features: This is the most common breed of dog owner. Dogs quickly learn the pattern of this owner, appearing to be somewhat obedient, then suddenly ignoring the owner's lengthy request to stay by his side. Instead the dog bolts across the street after a cat.

Giving your dog a lecture on what you'd like him to do simply creates a lack of focus for your dog. Dogs are movement-driven and action-oriented. Loosely translated: All talk and no guidance on the leash means your dog will misbehave, mainly because it can. This breed of dog owner says too much and means very little.

Bare-Bones Fact:

 PAW PRINT: Research has revealed that the act of petting a dog lowers a person's blood pressure.

**Think of obedience commands as letters of the alphabet
rather than entire sentences.**

The consistency of your own behavior is an important factor in
training your dog and achieving good communication. Identifying
your own personality among the seven breeds of dog owners enables you to see your own inconsistencies and address them before
your dog reacts to them. The following are seven bare-bones
people-training facts that apply to most circumstances and form
the foundation for positive development.

Seven Bare-Bones Facts of Training

1.   Your dog's training is only as good as the way you apply it.

2.   Your dog does not understand English, French, or Spanish—so
don't attempt to explain things ad nauseam. Match your tone to
the message you want to convey when training your dog.

3.   Think of obedience commands as letters of the alphabet rather
than entire sentences.

4.   Actions speak louder than looks.

5.   Obedience is the result of positive reinforcement, not discipline.

6.   Training should be incorporated into your daily routine.

7.   Don't beg or plead with your puppy. Learn how to guide him
on a leash to please you.

People training
A common quirk of couples is not being on the same page in
their puppy raising. Actress Leila Kenzle (*Mad about You*), a recov-
ering Coaxer, began slipping into a Whiner mode when her husband Neil, an admitted Control Freak, got a second dog, Maidie, a
Maltese. Peeing in the house was the problem. Although Neil
didn't like it, he thought that he had the situation under control.

Saying "Hey!" in a firm voice when he saw Maidie pee on the floor gave him the feeling of dedicated discipline while he was hoping that the pooch would eventually use the dog door and relieve herself outside. Poor Maidie was in a maze of confusion and still not using the dog door. While whining about the constant cleaning, Leila recognized she needed help and called me.

After I'd illustrated to them the different breeds of dog owners they had become, the issue was to get them both to concentrate on housebreaking Maidie by using the same approach: initiating "Outside" on a leash. I also showed them both how to reprimand their dog properly. (To learn how, see Chapter 6.)

Now that you have gotten a little insight into the different dog owner personalities, hopefully you're ready to appreciate how a new dog may feel trying to decode your behavior. As we identify and laugh at our own quirks, we gain understanding that should help eliminate some bad habits we have acquired. My teaching is about having foresight and clear communication, using reverse psychology, and being a little smarter than your dog.

All the Things You Need and Nothing More

Old Mother Hubbard
Went to the cupboard,
To get her dog a bone;
But when she came there
The cupboard was bare,
And so the poor dog had none.
—SARAH CATHERINE MARTIN

With the pet industry booming, it seems you need a master's degree in order to decide what to buy your pup. From doggy toothpaste to wee-wee pads, it can be hard to know what your dog really needs. To simplify the maze of merchandise sold in pet stores, I've created a shopping list for new dog owners.

The list indicates what you really need to ensure that your dog's needs are met. Here, too, I explain why you should purchase the listed items. In later chapters I will tell you how to use these tools and toys.

 PAW PRINT: The average owner spends close to $1,000 per year, not including health care, on his or her dog.

Shopping List for All the Things You Need and Nothing More

Most pet stores sell all of the following items:

Baby Gate or Corral

These come in different varieties and are sold in most pet stores. My favorite is the old-fashioned pressure gate with a wooden frame and a wire mesh front that fit most doorways.

Why a gate? In order to integrate your dog into your home, you need first to provide the pup with his special area. This gate helps you do that. (See Chapter 5, "Creating Positive Boundaries.")

Why a corral? Some houses have open areas, where the traditional baby gate does not fit in the doorway. In this case, a corral is the best option for creating a space. A corral, also known as an exercise pen, is an eight-paneled, freestanding wire fence that you can fold into different shapes, depending on the area you want to use for your pup. These pens are available in different heights at most pet stores.

Crate

If your puppy is young and still growing, get a crate big enough so that he can fit into it as an adult, especially if you want to use this crate later for travel or a doghouse. To estimate the adult size of your puppy, weigh him at four months of age and double that weight: if your pup weighs thirty pounds when he is four months old, he will grow to be approximately sixty pounds as an adult. (Again, see Chapter 5.)

What size crate should I buy? The crate should be big enough so your dog can comfortably turn around and lie down.

It should also be large enough to fit your dog as an adult. Don't buy a crate that will always be too big for your dog. (Don't put a Yorkshire terrier in a German Shepherd's crate.)

If you own a large-breed puppy and the crate is initially too big, block off half the crate with a cardboard box or an old pillow until your puppy grows into it.

What kind of crate is the best? A sky kennel, which is airline safe. Wire crates defeat the purpose of the den concept, which is to make a dark, cozy space that creates a sense of security for the puppy.

Why a crate? Dogs are den animals. They like to have a dark space to go into and rest. This helps a young puppy feel secure in a new environment. Later in training, being in a crate also teaches him to control his urge to go to the bathroom. (See Chapter 5.)

Bed

The purchase of a dog bed is a great alternative to allowing your dog to take over your couch. If your puppy is young and teething, save the bed until he is older.

Why wait? A dog bed is one of the first items people go out and buy, only to have it shredded while they are at the movies. This purchase can wait until after your dog is fully acclimated to your lifestyle. Until then, a couple of old beach towels fluffed into a makeshift bed will do the trick.

A Pair of Bowls

One food bowl and one water bowl.

Why? Your dog has to eat and drink from something! (Always make sure there is fresh water for Fido.)

Food: Dry Kibble or Canned?

What is the best food? There are many brands on the market. Most are up to standard, but it is best to ask your veterinarian for suggestions for your particular dog. However, dry food is thought to be best for keeping your dog's teeth and gums healthy and tartar free. I do not recommend canned food alone. If you want to use canned food as well as dry, then use only a small amount of the canned food and mix it in with the dry, as a flavor enhancer.

**Why is choosing the right food important?** If you do not do your research on what the best nutrients are for your growing pup or dog, it can cost you in the long run, with veterinary bills.

Leash

I prefer a leather flat leash, although nylon is also O.K. I do not recommend retractable leashes for training.

It's helpful to buy two leashes and keep one by the front door for in-home training purposes.

**Why a leash?** The leash is the only consistant way to guide your dog to understand basic obedience commands. Plus, you _must_ walk your dog.

Training Collar, a.k.a. Choke Chain or Slip Collar

The training collar, or choke chain, is a nylon or metal training collar. The links on the metal collar do not have to be large and either collar should slip over your pup's head. He may grow out of several collars during the course of his education. (See Chapter 4, Bare-Bones Basics.)

**Why this collar?** The choke chain is a very misunderstood training tool. It is not meant to choke your dog. You will use the collar with a leash to direct your dog to heel by quick snaps of the leash combined with a happy voice. (See Chapter 8, "Unleashing the Driver in You.")

Use this collar only for training. Do not leave a choke collar on a puppy when you are not training him.

Collar

This collar is made of either nylon or leather. It is worn to show name tag and registration. This should be thought of as the dog's permanent collar. Make sure to adjust your puppy's collar as he grows.

**Why a permanent collar?** Your dog needs to wear a collar with proper identification at all times, in case he gets lost. It should have a tag with your address and phone number and also a dog license tag on it.

Tags and Dog License

Name tag: Very important. You should order this from a pet store immediately. Tags usually take a couple of weeks to be made. It is a good idea to order two tags in case the first one gets lost or falls off, which has been known to happen. Temporary name tags can be purchased until the permament one comes in the mail.

Dog license: This is required by law for pups four months and older. You can get dog licenses and tags from shelters and your local animal regulations office. You must provide a current certificate for all vaccinations. The license must be renewed yearly.

Why are they important? They are like your dog's driver's license and ID. If he gets lost without a name tag on his collar, both of you are out of luck.

Tennis Ball

A great exercise tool.

Squeaky Toy

The squeaky toy noise might give you a headache but this is a fun toy and really cute for puppies.

Why? Squeaky toys provide great stimulation for young puppies. Unfortunately, however, some pups and adolescent dogs will chew them to pieces. If your dog does this, take the toy away.

Rawhide

The most frequently asked questions regarding rawhide are, "What is it?" and "Is it good for your dog?" It is actually made from the hide of a cow or buffalo. Some people feel that it is too hard for their dog to digest and therefore harmful. There are many types of rawhide, on the market and the best kind to get is pressed rawhide, which is unbleached and a natural light brown in color. Rawhide comes in bone shapes and sticks. Rawhide chips are also available, but they are too small and thin; they can get stuck in a dog's throat.

<u>*Why?*</u> Dogs—especially young ones—need to chew. Unless your dog has a particular digestive ailment, rawhide is a godsend and certainly more digestible than a shoe or a couch. Large bone and stick shapes are the best.

> **Caution: Keep a watchful eye. If the piece of rawhide your dog chews begins to get too small, throw it away.**

Pig's Ears

Yes, they are actually the ears of a pig. As disgusting as they may seem, dogs savor them. They can be bought individually or by the dozen. The ear is thin enough to satisfy a young puppy's teething urge and is a boon for puppies ten weeks to five months and up. Older dogs eat them like potato chips.

 PAW PRINT: The first Lassie was actually a male dog, named Pal, who was bought for $10.

Chewy Rolls

A part of the bull's anatomy that I would rather not talk about, but dogs love them. Long-lasting and digestible, and a terrific chew item for adolescent dogs.

Hooves

This chew item is suited for the older puppy and all dogs. Long-lasting and not very expensive.

Carrot Bones

A vegetarian alternative to the bone. Carrot bones are actually made with carrots and are a little too hard for a puppy that still has its baby teeth, but great for dogs six months old and up. There are also spinach, potato, and other flavors.

Hard Rubber Teething Ring

Great for dogs of all ages.

Treats

The best dog treats to give your puppy are dog biscuits or any kind of *doggy* beef jerky or liver treats. These can be found in all pet supply stores.

WARNING: Some treats can kill your dog.

Do NOT feed your dog chocolate or any human cookies or ice cream. Chocolate contains a caffeine-like alkaloid called theobromine that is very toxic to dogs. This can make your dog very sick and even kill your dog. Likewise, sugar of any kind is not a treat for your dog; it is very harmful.

Chicken bones and other restaurant leftovers can also be dangerous. I will make no bones about this: Chicken bones, steak bones, and similar delicacies can splinter and lodge in your dog's throat and/or stomach lining and kill your dog.

Bitter Apple

This is a bad-tasting spray or cream that is an aid used to stop puppies from chewing on furniture during their teething stage. Spray cabinets and table legs to safeguard against accidental destruction. Bitter Apple is safe for puppies and won't harm finished wood.

Nature's Miracle

A solution that removes urine stains and eliminates odor. A must for surviving puppyhood.

Now that you've bought the basics, it's time to put them to work.

Bare-Bones Basics

Knowledge is power.
—FRANCIS BACON

Many people feel frustrated because their new puppy does not behave like a well-mannered adult dog. Some expect their dog to recite the alphabet in Latin at the age of four months. What they need to realize is that certain puppy behavior is completely normal. Dog-owner confidence comes from knowing what is typical behavior and what is not suitable at any given stage of a puppy's growth. False expectations as to how fast your pup can retain training may mar your experience, not to mention ruin a happy relationship. Make no bones about it, I am all for an early education. Granted, we all have very bright dogs, but we need to take training one step at a time, at least for the dog's sake.

Therefore, in this chapter I have outlined five stages of doggy development, to give you an overview of what to expect over the first two years of raising a pooch. Even if your pet is not a pup, this overview will help you gauge what stage your dog is in before you attempt to tackle the training process. Remember, it is never too late to educate your dog. Age is not a factor. It is up to *you* to unleash your pooch's potential.

I will also address the concept of the training collar, a.k.a. the choke chain, and give you the real scoop on this corrective tool. You'll find out how, when, and why you should use a training collar on your pup and at what age it is best to begin teaching your dog.

Confidence comes with knowing the stages of development of your dog, no matter what the temperament. So if you are in love with your new pup, but he is driving you crazy, you are not alone. Before you begin housebreaking your dog and dealing with the teething stage, it's helpful to know what stage of development your puppy is in. The following overview of the five stages of doggy development should help in matching your expectations with your dog's biological needs.

STAGES OF DOGGY DEVELOPMENT

Stage One: Eight Weeks to Three Months—Infant Puppy

This is the angel stage. Your puppy is sleeping, eating, playing, and pooping. Although the first few nights may be noisy, generally your puppy can do no wrong.

People-training tip: Most people believe their puppy is Einstein. Be careful—your wonder child may turn into your wild child.

Stage Two: Three to Five Months—Toddler

Your puppy has a license to be Jaws. Baby teeth are falling out and new adult teeth are growing in. He should be very alert and eager to grasp the step-by-step process of housebreaking and training with your guidance, although teething and immaturity can get in the way. Remember, this radical change for your pup takes place in only two or three months. So keep the pig's ears and chewy rolls coming.

During this period, your puppy should learn to hold the urge to go to the bathroom all night long. The series of vaccination shots should be completed. Basic training begins now.

The formal obedience commands—"Heel," "Sit," "Stay," "Down," and "Come"—can begin to be applied as early as three months of age. Remember, this formal training is like teaching your dog his ABCs. The process begins with applying the techniques on a leash, in the comfortable setting of your home. The biggest mistake people make is trying too much too soon with a pup or trying to apply commands without a leash.

People-training tip: Patience is a virtue.

Stage Three: Six Months to One Year—Adolescence

This teenage stage has its own obstacles. I call this the "Baby Hughy" stage. Your puppy, if a large breed, looks like he's all grown up, but he is still just a teenager. His adult teeth are in, but his need to chew can still be voracious. *You need to spay or neuter your dog at this time.*

Training should be taking shape, still applied on a leash. This is the stage where the kinks should be worked out in training and in housebreaking. You will clearly see what is good behavior, and be ready to tackle the bad habits that might arise. (See Chapter 11, "Working Out the Kinks.")

People adopting adult dogs from shelters should start at stage three, no matter what the estimated age of the rescued dog. Dogs from shelters have unknown backgrounds and need extra training and focus in order to acclimate properly to you and your home.

People-training tip: Take a deep breath and work out the kinks.

Stage Four: One to Two Years—Young Adult

Once you have worked out the kinks, you and your dog are ready for advanced obedience. The process will ultimately depend on your dog's temperament, your guidance, and your chemistry together. Hopefully, during this stage you will find yourself in a groove with your dog. Chew toys and bones are still necessary, but your dog should be fully housebroken and trustworthy while loose in the house.

People-training tip: By this time, you've decided whether you're happy with your dog-communication skills, or whether you are going on to study at Harvard. Some dog owners continue training to the level of off-leash obedience, some do not.

Stage Five: Two Years Old and Up—Adult

Your dog is emotionally and physically mature. Well, you made it! You've achieved Lassie. From here on out, your dog is totally in tune with your schedule and lifestyle.

People-training tip: At this point, most people have a selective memory about the process of training, depending on what their experience was like. They may want to rock the boat by following an urge to add a second dog.

> Remember, if you a adopt an adult dog from a shelter, you should start the process at stage three, regardless of its age. I want to emphasize this point because all new dogs (not just puppies) need guidance and boundaries in a new home.

BASIC COMMUNICATION

It's true, training your dog does require repetition and consistency. However, repetition alone is not going to do the trick. Basic communication with your new puppy requires a leash. Most people try to convince their dog to behave. Although their energy is in the right place, without a leash their words are just babble to the dog.

All dogs want to please, they just may not know how. Guiding them on a leash, establishing rules, and creating a routine to meet their needs (e.g., what to chew and when and where go to the bathroom) will structure their time and avoid destructive behavior. Trying to control your dog verbally only allows certain behaviors to happen in the first place. Loving and learning do not have to be two different things. Talk to your dog all you want, just don't try to implement basic commands off leash until your dog knows the basics on leash. This would be like trying to graduate from college without knowing the alphabet.

The Regular Collar

The first step is to get your pup used to wearing a regular nylon collar, while supervised. Be careful with young puppies. Make sure there is nothing the collar could get caught on, especially if you're leaving your pup unattended. (If in doubt, take off the collar when you are not at home.) Your puppy might scratch a lot at first, because the collar feels unfamiliar. Your puppy will get used to it in a short time.

Put name tags on the nylon or leather collar right away. Get your pup used to the feel of a leash by walking him around your living room. While walking, use a squeaky toy to distract your pup from fretting about being on a leash for the first time. Once this is accomplished, you are ready to try the training collar.

CAUTION: Do not leave a collar on an infant puppy when you are not home. It could get caught on something and choke the pup.

The Training Collar: What, When, Where, Why, and How

The training collar, also called a choke chain, is very misunderstood. Many people think of this collar as a torture device and refuse to use it. Others use it, but often do so incorrectly. Whether you own a Great Dane or a Maltese, the training collar is a teaching tool.

The collar is made from chain or nylon cord and slips over the dog's neck like a necklace. Your dog should not look like Mr. T. wearing a big chain. The collar should fit over the dog's head and hang slightly below his neckline. A nylon or lightweight chain is good for toy breeds. A light-to-medium-weight chain is best for most other breeds. If you have a young dog, you may have to buy several sizes as he grows.

The number one fear of all new dog owners is that the training collar will hurt their dog or choke him. The funny thing is that most young dogs I see walking down the street, untrained and wearing regular collars, are choking as they pull their owners along.

The training collar is used in teaching your pup to walk at your speed and to focus as you communicate commands with quick snaps of the leash. Dogs will find this process fun, if you set a precedent by having confidence in your actions. Just like learning to ride a bike, it can be scary until you get used to it.

When should you use a training collar?

Get your pup walking on a leash at three and a half or four months old. First, walk him using a regular nylon collar. Speak with a happy, upbeat tone of voice. Once your pup is successfully walking with you, try the same process using the training collar instead of the nylon one. The same goes for older dogs, too. You should use a training collar for daily walks and while teaching your dog.

Where should you begin to use the training collar?

The best place to start is in your living room or around the house for 5 or 10 minutes at a time. Begin training your pup indoors first, mainly because there is less distraction than outdoors. Dogs are pack animals and love to follow the leader. A young puppy should gladly follow you on a leash, if you make it fun with your voice.

You might feel odd about putting your dog on a leash in the house. However, this is the best place to achieve success. If your pup has never been on a leash before, getting him used to feeling the weight of the leash and following you around the house is a big achievement. When this is accomplished, you can try going on walks outside.

Why should you use the training collar?

The training collar teaches your dog to focus on you and not to pull while on a leash. A quick little snap of the leash tightens and releases the collar, indicating to your dog to pay attention. Putting your new puppy on a leash and training collar can sometimes be trying, depending on his temperament. Some pups have no trouble at all and are willing to follow you; others are stubborn. If your pup rebels, take baby steps and stick with it.

How to put on the training collar
Some of the brightest people I know have a problem with this, so don't worry about feeling stupid.

• The training collar is a length of chain with a large ring at either end. Hold one of the rings and slide the middle of the chain through the ring so it makes a loop. Presto, it's a loop that makes a collar.

• Hold up the loop so it is facing you. The collar should make the shape of the letter P facing you.

• Place your dog in front of you and slide the loop over the dog's head. (Making the letter P with the chain is important because, when your dog walks on your left, the loop will momentarily tighten when the leash is snapped and then loosened. If you put on the collar incorrectly, the collar will not loosen after a snap.)

• Attach the leash to the ring on your left-hand side as you *face your dog*.

Once the leash and training collar are on, you are ready to rock and roll. Try walking around your apartment or house.

Bare-Bones Basics

• Place your pup on your left side.

• Hold the leash in your right hand while walking.

• To stop, slide your left hand to the clasp on the leash and pull up and down on the leash and say "Sit."
The quick snaps of the training collar along with the sound of

your voice will indicate to your dog what you want him to do, such as sit or heel alongside you.

• Once your dog sits, then with another couple quick snaps of the leash and with a happy voice say "Let's go" and take a few steps. Walk around the house so that you can both get into the rhythm of walking together without too many distractions. When you stop and guide your dog to sit, you will begin to notice that your dog is looking up at you. This is the eye contact and focus you want to begin to see. Remember, this is not discipline or boot camp. Try to keep your voice light and happy.

How Do You Use the Training Collar?
Say "Let's go" and take several steps forward while giving a few snaps of the leash. At first, take only a few steps at a time. If your puppy is struggling, take along a squeaky toy and squeeze it

TAIL WAG: LEILA KENZLE
"Choke chain! On my dog! I just spent a million dollars on everything my dog needs and now you want me to choke him!" This was the re-action of actress Leila Kenzle. Her dog Bill, a small poodle, had trou-ble walking down the street without pulling, coughing, and gagging on a regular collar. For Leila, taking a stroll with Bill became his Emmy Award–winning performance, rather than a nice walk. People would stop Leila to ask if her dog was all right. He wasn't even wearing a choke chain, only a regular nylon collar. When she took Bill to a vet, the cause of his antics was diagnosed: emotional. She called me, des-perate to solve this problem. Bill's dilemma was that outside walks were so exciting and anxiety-ridden that he would almost suffer a panic attack while pulling Leila down the street. Getting Bill used to walking around with the training collar and leash on in the house shifted his attention to pleasing Leila. The combination of quick snaps of the leash and verbal encouragement, using the word "Heel" and taking a few steps at a time, redirected Bill's focus from pulling to prancing next to her. The gagging and coughing stopped. Leila is again the main actor in the house.

while walking, to gain his focus. Then stop and ask your dog to "Sit" by lifting up the leash. If he does not sit, just repeat "Sit" and lift up on the leash, then release it, repeating this pattern until he sits. Keep your voice nice.

Training your new puppy to walk on a leash is just like singing the alphabet to a young child. There is no discipline involved, just positive reinforcement. Have patience. Repetition is the key.

If you are having difficulty and your puppy begins to yelp as if you are hurting him, don't panic. He is most likely telling you to jump in the lake because he is just not used to being led on a leash. This collar does not hurt your dog, if you use it properly. Holding a treat or a toy while walking may temporarily distract your puppy from remembering he is on a leash and wearing a training collar.

CAUTION: The choke chain is only a training collar. Do not allow your young puppy to wear a choke chain unattended.

Creating Positive Boundaries

Nothing succeeds like success.
—ALEXANDRE DUMAS

MOVING IN TOGETHER

A commitment has been made, you're a new dog owner. The camera comes out, friends come over, and the party begins. You profess that you are in love. The intoxication of puppy love is wonderful, and everything your pooch does is just plain O.K. with you.

However, most new dog owners experience a feeling of panic at least once during the first seventy-two hours of owning their new pup. Questions creep up: "Where should my new little angel sleep?" or "What if I want to leave?" Such thoughts are usually followed by statements like "I am not going to put my new dog in a crate all night and lock the door. That's mean!" Many people adopt a permissive let's-see-if-the-puppy-will-be-okay-in-the-house-while-we-go-to-the-movies attitude. This can lead to big trouble. These first few days of learning to live with a new pooch can evoke a roller coaster of emotions for a new dog parent.

The information in this chapter will help you create the foundation for your dog's security and a base for the housebreaking process. Many new pups suffer from separation anxiety. Even longtime furry family members stress out when their owners leave. Sometimes this nervousness can lead to destruction, not to mention dog-owner anxiety. Having to squeeze your body through the door and physically push your dog back in order to leave can be distressing for you—and your dog. The process of gating teaches your dog to wait in his own area and, over time, reduces separation anxiety and gives owners peace of mind. Gating your new pup in a given area is a valuable procedure that will create trust, on which all good friendships are built.

For people-training purposes I have defined four stages of cohabitation to explain how to make your pup feel safe and secure in his new home. This guide will give you the confidence and understanding that you need to fit your new dog into your lifestyle. But first, let's look at the things you should *not* do with your pup the first day.

Nine Things You Should *Not* Do with Your Dog the First Day

1.   Do not bring your new dog home and then leave. Plan to hang out with your dog the first day and evening. Although this suggestion sounds like basic common sense, many people do not thoroughly plan out this first day of owning their pooch. They leave, do a quick errand, and come home to destruction.

2.   Do not expect your shelter dog to be fully housebroken or to be free of separation anxiety just because he is an adult dog.

3.   Do not feed your dog table scraps. You are not being kind. Think how your stomach feels when you are nervous, scared, and in a strange place.

4.   Do not let other household pets approach the new pup the first day. Keep them separated with a baby gate for the first week. That way they can smell each other through the gate, yet not feel threatened by the other pet or pets invading their territory.

5.   Do not let your new pooch play with other dogs the first day. It is overwhelming to meet your new parents and new home and be sniffed over by new dogs, too!

6.   Do not take a very young puppy to the park the first day. Your pup can get very sick. Your puppy must have all of his shots before he goes outside. Ask your veterinarian. Believe me, it's better to be safe than sorry.

7.   If you have children, do not let them handle a new puppy excessively the first day. (See Chapter 13, "Having It All.")

8.   Do not allow your new puppy to sleep with you in bed. If you do this, he will have a hard time learning to be by himself. What are you going to do when you go to work? When your dog is trained, finished teething, and fully housebroken, he can sleep wherever you want.

9.   Do not allow a young puppy to roam freely at all times in your house. Create an area for your puppy to call its own. Designate free time in the house when you are able to play with him and keep an eye on him.

O.K., so now you're probably thinking, "What *can* I do with my puppy the first few days?" The first day, many people wait to see how their dog is going to behave. Others try to coax their new puppy to behave.

Paws for a minute and think about this . . .
You wouldn't allow your human baby to crawl around the floor without diapers for hours and get into mischief, then start yelling "No!" at it. So why allow your puppy to do the same? Most people let their new pooch run around loose without supervision until it gets into things, and then they scream "No!" repeatedly. When you say "No!" you must think, "No, what?" Don't be a puppy? This only emphasizes the negative. A lot of pups, depending on their stage of development, get into one kind of mischief or another. After the third day some new pups begin to think their names are "Uh-uh!" "Hey!" or "No! Bad Dog." This chapter will

give new dog parents the guidance they need to create a foundation of emotional security with their pet. Even if we have owned dogs before, we sometimes have selective memory in recalling those first few days. Keep in mind, too, that every relationship is different.

The following four stages of cohabitation are what all new dog owners go through during the first three days of having a new dog, whether they have owned a dog before or not.

Stage One: Infatuation

Infatuation is the first stage for every new dog parent. Your puppy can do no wrong. He or she can redecorate in ways that would shock Martha Stewart, pee on the floor, chew your best shoes—nothing seems more adorable to a new dog parent, at least for the first day. Despite your very large Visa bill for all the necessary doggie items, the pup usually has full rein to play with everything in the house or apartment. In this stage of puppy parenting it is most important to create a space for your pup. Creating a space will give him the security blanket he needs to feel safe in his new environment. It will also give you peace of mind.

Stage Two: The Stunned Factor

The stunned factor applies to both people and pups, and sometimes even neighbors. For many new dog owners, the hours leading to bedtime can be nerve-wracking. Your puppy may be singing the blues. You're tired and you realize your life, as you knew it, is gone. Things have changed drastically.

You are praying that the pup is going to be pooped enough to sleep. Feeling a little like Cinderella after the ball, you clean up another mess, amazed that such a small dog can go to the bathroom so often. You need to know where your new pup should sleep and why.

Stage Three: Uncertainty

Feelings of deep uncertainty surface. You have graduated from "What have I done?" to "What am I going to do with my pup when I leave for work?" During stage three you learn that you need to prepare your pup to be alone at home for the first time.

Stage Four: Responsibility

By the third day, you can't remember what it was like living without dog slobber. Coming home from work has new meaning, with your new friend so happy to welcome you. There are routines to establish and a schedule to keep. You begin to feel prepared to guide your puppy, rather than follow him.

The day you bring your new dog home is exciting and a little scary, for both of you. Most new dog parents gush over their new puppy and don't create any boundaries. Allowing your pet to roam all over the house and follow you all the time can create a very insecure puppy. This can lead to a multitude of problems, including codependence. Codependent behavior arises when your dog derives his security from your physical presence, rather than from positive boundaries.

Years ago, I trained Jim Carrey's family dog Carl, a Jack Russell, who was shy and had to be housebroken. Like a child, this four-month-old terrier needed a daily routine and his own area to feel safe and secure while he chewed on bones. Gating built his confidence and helped curb separation anxiety problems.

Gating helped teach Kevin Costner's dog Wyatt to wait, and not jump out the car window. The "Wait" command is an important part of the gating routine. Teaching dogs and their owners to distinguish between the commands "Wait" (hang out in this area) and "Stay" (stay in one spot) is important for future lifestyle uses.

CREATING YOUR PUP'S OWN SPACE

Teach your dog to wait behind a baby gate. It is best to create a space for him in a central part of your home, where family members hang out. Use baby gates or a corral (a multipaneled pen) to partition a part of a room. Put all of the pup's new toys in that space. Sit in the gated area with your dog and play with him there. This applies to older dogs from a shelter as well.

There should be no carpeting in the pup's new area. If you live in an apartment, you might want to gate the kitchen or a hallway, so the dog can still see you as you move around. It is reassuring to the pup to see that you are not abandoning him as he gets acclimated to his new area.

Think of the dog's gated area as a playpen, not solitary confinement. Initially your pup will be unhappy with any form of containment. There will be some crying. This is normal for the first three days. Although this period is taxing, know that shutting a door on a new dog or putting him in a remote part of the house— or leaving him in the backyard—causes even more anxiety.

When you bring your new pup home, set up his space right away. Make sure all his needs are met, such as being fed and having plenty of water and chew bones and toys. For an infant pup, put papers down at one end of the gated area, in case he needs to eliminate. For an older one, guide him outside on a leash to go potty. For the first few days, housebreaking your pup will be a hit-or-miss affair. (This topic is covered at length in the next chapter.) For now, the first step is guiding your pup to be calm and comfortable in his new space.

The gated area will be your pup's room for many months. The main purpose for this area is to teach your dog boundaries. All dogs suffer from anxiety when they arrive in a new home. It's simply not fair, no matter how old the dog is, to introduce him into your home and let him fend for himself. Your first mission is to teach your dog not to have separation anxiety. Gating helps accomplish this.

If you don't create any boundaries and you allow a new dog to follow you around all day, then when you want to leave (and you eventually *will* have to leave the house for one reason or another), your dog will suffer from separation anxiety. To prevent this you need to gate your dog while you are at home. That way he will get used to seeing you while gated and realize that he will not automatically be left alone when gated.

How Long Should My Puppy Stay Gated the First Day?

Begin by gating your pooch for twenty minutes the first day. Stay with him in the gated area. The idea is to gradually extend the dog's time in the playpen from twenty minutes to forty minutes to an hour on up. The goal is to eventually be able to gate your pup and leave for work and not have him feel abandoned, but this could take a few days.

Certainly you can have free time with your dog in the house, outside of the gated area, but make sure the pup is supervised the whole time.

It is very important to exercise your pup and tire him out before putting him back in the gated area. Not unlike children, puppies need to be guided on when to play and when to chill out, what they may chew, and when they should nap. They actually want to have clarity on how to please you.

It is important to understand that gating promotes a sense of emotional security for your dog, if done correctly. Giving a new dog too much space can result in many chewing and peeing accidents. Then people enforce boundaries as a form of reprimand. **Do not implement boundaries as a form of punishment.**

Creating positive boundaries for your dog is no different from setting up a schedule for a child. You would not say to a young child, "Here are the house keys, come and go as you please." Structure aids children in establishing good patterns for life. Likewise, boundaries assist your dog and you in developing a workable and loving relationship.

The gated area should remain your dog's playpen or room until the time he is fully housebroken and past his teething stage. This could take anywhere from up to a month or as long as eight months, depending on your individual circumstance.

Choosing a Location

Regardless of your dog's age, the following are the best areas in your house to baby-gate him.

- Kitchen area
- A laundry room, if it's not too remote
- A bathroom off your bedroom
- A portion of a hallway

Note: Make sure the area is not carpeted.

Things to Put in the Puppy Area

- A sky kennel crate. Take off the door of the crate so that your puppy can roam in and out of the crate as he wishes.
- Towels to make the crate cushy
- A bowl of water
- Chew bones and toys

Note: For puppies that are eight weeks to four months old, put down newspapers on the floor at the opposite end from the crate. When a puppy is four months old, take up all newspapers for good. (See Chapter 6, "How to Get Your Dog Not to Pee in Your House.")

Leading Your Dog *into* the Gated Area

1.   Put your puppy on a leash.

2.   Guide him into the gated area with a happy voice, saying "Let's go."

3.   Take your time and tell your pup to sit by gently lifting up on the leash, saying "Sit" in a nice voice. If your dog looks at you like you are from another planet, he is not being stubborn or afraid, he just doesn't know what you want from him. This can also be awkward for you because you are guiding him to do something for the first time. Repeat lifting up on the leash while saying the word

"Sit" until he does sit. With a new puppy this requires a gentle touch and lots of patience.

4.   Then say "Wait" and back up, leaving him in the area where you want him to wait. Still holding the leash, back out of the gated area and put up the baby gate.

If your pup tries to bolt through the doorway, guess what? He's on a leash, and you can stop him and say "No! No! No!" Then repeat "Sit" and "Wait" and put up the gate.

5.   Take off the leash and go about your business for twenty minutes or so. The first day you gate your pup, hang out just outside of the gated area, reading or having a cup of coffee.

Keep your new pup in the area for twenty minutes at a time, slowly increasing the amount of time, leading to bedtime.

> **It is very important to remove your puppy's collar when he's gated. Also make sure you dog-proof the gated area and remove any cleaning detergents, electrical cords, telephone wires, and other possible hazzards.**

Leading Your Dog *out* of the Gated Area

1.   Put on the leash.

2.   Say "Sit. Wait."

3.   Remove the baby gate, while repeating the command "Wait" in a pleasant voice. If he tries to bolt through the doorway, put the gate down and say "No! No! No!" in a firm voice. Say "Sit. Wait." in a nice voice.

4.   Get eye contact by drawing your hand up to your eyes and saying the word "O.K." Guide him through the doorway. Go directly outside from the gated area, saying the word "Outside," signaling to your dog that you want him to go to the bathroom.

Remember that gating your pooch lets him see you through the baby gate and over time creates a safe place for him.

Some pups scream when gated or left alone for the first time, some destroy things looking for a way out, and some are plain O.K. It depends largely on your dog's temperament and also on how you guide him to behave the first day. Try to relax and have fun and play with your pup, but don't be an overachiever dog parent. You cannot teach your new pup everything in the first few days.

Bedtime Stories

On the first night, exhaust your pup by letting him chase a ball. Then put him in the gated area a couple of hours prior to going to sleep and sit with him. Occasionally, walk out of the room and come back. Just prior to going to bed yourself, take him outside for his final potty break. Then guide him back into his space for the night and give him a pig's ear to chew, which should also help tire him.

Like children, some pups are more difficult than others. Those that are more anxious may require greater patience, as well as soft music or a night light. If your pup starts to whine or cry, don't panic. Your pup may cry for several reasons. Some cry at 2 A.M. because they are announcing to the world that they need to go to the bathroom. Others are just scared because they are in a new place. It usually takes about three days for a new dog to adjust to its space.

If crying persists, from out of sight say a firm "No!" Then repeat the command "Wait" a few times in a pleasant voice. Remain out of view for a couple of minutes, then return and sit with your pup quietly for a short time, gently stroking him with the lights out.

Do not succumb and allow your new puppy to sleep with you. For his own emotional stability, your dog needs to develop independence from you. Later, when he is older and well trained, he can sleep on your bed, if you like. But if you cave in now, prepare for your neighbors' wrath, because he will definitely cry and yelp whenever you leave him alone.

Pound Pups

Many shelter dogs appear to be easier to handle because they are adopted as adults. However, the same procedure should apply when introducing one of them into a new home. Chances are the dog did not have an ideal puppyhood or he would not have ended up in the shelter in the first place.

A rescued dog can have more baggage—meaning separation anxiety and other issues—that might take time to surface. It's best to bring your new dog home from the shelter on a weekend, so that you have two full days to bond with him. A rescued dog, regardless of the estimated age, must also be given boundaries. No matter how placid and easygoing the dog may seem, it behooves you to start guiding him from day one in your home. Giving your dog too much space may result in many chewing and peeing accidents.

Remember, he or she could have been in the shelter for a number of reasons—whether because the dog was not raised properly, or ran away, or because destructive behavior was never successfully addressed and the dog was abandoned. Whatever the reason, do not assume that the personality you see in the shelter is going to indicate the dog's behavior in your home.

People who adopt adult dogs often do so under the false assumption that their dog is already housebroken, and they think there is no need for any boundaries. Rescued dogs have unknown upbringings. Therefore they require special patience and handling. Many people have a problem with this because they feel it is cruel to gate a dog that comes from a caged environment like a shelter (or a pet store). But remember, many dogs from city shelters, had to defecate in their dog run. Therefore, housebreaking, even for an older dog, must be formalized and taught in your home.

You want your puppy to derive his sense of security from the routine and positive boundaries you establish, not your physical presence.

Jumping over the Gate

For some pups, abandonment issues are acute, so extra care is needed in order to socialize them in a gated area. Rescued dogs are trickier, since there is no telling what their issues may be, or how they are going to adapt. Some dogs freak out and jump over the gate. If this happens, have patience.

If the dog has a lot of anxiety and jumps over the gate, imagine what he would do in your backyard or if shut off in a room. By following the steps of gating in this chapter, you'll find your dog will acclimate slowly to his new space, and the process will build trust between you and the dog. This is one reason it is important to gate your dog the first day when you are at home, and especially before bedtime. The gating procedure for a rescued dog is exactly the same as for a new puppy.

If your dog jumps over the gate, get a coffee can, empty it, put a handful of pennies in it, and close the lid. Now you have a penny can. Get the leash, put it on your dog, and walk him back into his area, saying, in a nice voice, "Let's go." Tell your dog to "Sit" by pulling up on the leash, then put up the gate again. Get ready to give a surprise shake of the penny can and say "No!" firmly if he tries to jump up over the gate again. This is done not to be mean, but to clearly define that he should not jump over the gate, period.

In extreme cases, if your dog persistently jumps over the gate, you can put one baby gate on top of the other in the doorway. Using two gates prevents your dog from physically getting over the gates. After several hours of being gated, take him outside then have free time (loose in the house with you), which will establish a routine. Use the double gates intermittently for a couple of days, and when the anxiety of trying to get over the gate has subsided, you can try the same process with one gate. Remember, if your dog is on a mission to escape from the gated area, just think what he would do to your front door if he was left loose when you leave for work.

Gating creates a precedent for the dog so that he will be able to chill out and relax when you are not home. Otherwise, in time behaviors such as digging, excessive barking, ripping up your furniture may develop—all out of boredom and a lack of boundaries or direction. This way you are directing your dog to relax. Once destructive behavior has developed, it is harder for both you and your dog to establish these boundaries. It's better to take vitamins before you get sick.

Practice Leaving

Take the penny can with you and practice leaving for the first time. But don't really leave. If your dog tries to jump over the gate, shake the penny can once and say "No!" from the doorway and then in a nice voice say "Wait." Try leaving again. The first time you actually do leave, only run a short errand. The next few trips can be longer, as your pup adjusts. This process builds trust.

   People-training tip: Leave music on when you leave. It sets a routine for your dog.

SEPARATION ANXIETY

Shutting a door on any new dog can create a lot of anxiety for the dog, not to mention your own anxiety, listening to the sound of your door being redesigned by the dog scratching on it to get out. Before long, this stressful situation escalates until you've developed a full-blown bad habit of physically pushing back your dog and then shutting the door in his face.

TAIL WAG: LEANN RIMES
Is your pup singing the blues because he's gated for the first time in a new home? Well, you're not alone. Every new puppy parent has gone through this the first night, including my client, Grammy Award—winning singer LeAnn Rimes. Her five-month old Pomeranian pup, Raven, had to get used to traveling with her when she went on tour. A combination of gating and crating helped prepare him to be housebroken in different environments and accustomed to her temporary absence. After the second day, with a little patience, Raven's crying stopped. Now, Raven can be happily gated or crated when LeAnn is busy. He is well on his way to being housebroken and trained. All of our dogs should be lucky enough to have such a lullaby!

For the dog, the stress of trying to squeeze through a door being closed on him can make him very anxious when you leave. This is one of the main reasons gating is so important. Gating your dog allows him to see you through the gate and not feel shut off by a door closing in his face. The gate reduces stress and creates a nice ritual of sitting and hanging out with you in the same vicinity. Make sure you always guide him into the gated area on the leash, then take the leash off once the gate is up.

TO CRATE OR NOT TO CRATE?
THAT IS THE QUESTION

Contrary to popular practice, I do *not* recommend crating your dog all night for the first few weeks, unless your new dog is already used to sleeping in a crate. Baby-gating can be an alternative to crating overnight, yet many dog owners are not even aware of this concept as an option. A crate is a fine idea if your dog is accustomed to it, and is at least four months old. The crate method is basically a phase of housebreaking, which will be discussed at length in the next chapter.

If your puppy has never been in a crate before, I would recommend leaving the crate, with its door off, in the gated area for a few weeks. This allows your pup to go in and out of the crate on his own and get used to it without fear of being closed off. Later, the crate door having shut will not be traumatic. Crating sets a pattern for your dog to relax when you are resting. During the housebreaking process, the crate can be moved to different parts of your house, teaching your dog to hold his urge to eliminate and to know the route outside. But for now, our mission is to just introduce the crate concept to our dog by getting him used to it within the gated area.

Pre-crating

1.   Create a space in your kitchen or laundry room (make sure the area is not too remote).

2.   Take the door off the crate for a couple of weeks.

3.   Put the crate at one end of your puppy's gated area.

4.   Spread out newspapers at the opposite end of the gated area.

5.   Put towels (as cushions) and toys in the crate.

Remember, the crate will represent a cozy den space, providing a sense of security for your dog. In time, he will go into the crate and hang out.

The idea goes like this: Your puppy won't defecate where it sleeps. Crating teaches your pup to hold it for a number of hours. Be aware of the pup's age. Keep in mind that an eight- or ten-week-old puppy can't physically hold it eight hours. Crating a new young pup is rather traumatic if the pup is not used to going in and out of a crate on his own first. When your pup is four months old, it is anatomically ready to hold it through the night. By that time he will be accustomed to relaxing in his crate within the gated area with the crate door open.

When he seems comfortable and relaxed in the crate, your pup can be locked in the crate all night long and moved to your bedroom or another part of the house. This teaches him to hold the urge to go to the bathroom in different areas of the house, and learn the route outside. In the morning, *guide your pup outside on a leash from the crate* and make sure he actually eliminates.

Think of the crate as your dog's own private condo. Condo, *not* confinement. Innately, dogs derive a sense of security from a den. If you don't provide a crate for your puppy, he will make his own den by sleeping underneath a coffee table, but he won't learn to hold it.

Never push your dog into the crate and shut the door. Always socialize your dog to the crate in gradual stages.

 PAW PRINT: In 1916, Stubby, a homeless mutt, was enlisted into the U.S. Armed Forces. He alerted soldiers of coming attacks, was on the front line, caught a German spy, and even served as therapy for visiting wounded soldiers.

How to Crate Your Dog

1. After a few weeks of letting the crate serve as a dog bed in the gated area, put the door back on the crate.

2. Always guide your dog into the crate on a leash. Say "Wait," take the leash and training collar off, and shut the door.

3. Initially, shut the dog in the crate for twenty minutes at a time. If everything is fine and your dog does not seem anxious, then increase crating time gradually to several hours. Make sure he has a rawhide or carrot bone to chew. Eventually, your dog can be crated all night long.

4. The key to crating is always to use a leash while guiding the dog out of the crate and take him directly outside. Open the crate door, say "Sit. Wait," then "O.K.," and guide your dog outside. If you crate a dog overnight and let him out without putting on the leash to guide him, the whole purpose is defeated. Your dog will have held it and, on the way outside, may decide to go to the bathroom in the nearest hallway. You need to guide him outside to relieve himself.

Right now the main point of gating or crating is that your dog should be socialized to the space for short periods of time while you are at home. Gradually increase the time. This will reduce any initial anxiety until your dog learns that this is his space, a den. Later, it will also serve as a step in housebreaking your dog. Plus, it reduces your stress, since you'll know your pup is safe.

 PAW PRINT: Within 3 weeks of birth, all of your dog's senses are functioning at full capacity.

People don't want to train their dogs if they think they have to be mean or tough. Yet these same people may have no problem disciplining their dogs because of constant unruly behavior. This all changes when you realize that dogs, like children, need positive boundaries. If positive boundaries are set first, negative patterns never get started.

Keep reading and find out how these boundaries will help you teach your pup not to pee in your house.

How to Get Your Dog Not to Pee in Your House

Lord, grant me patience, and I want it
right now.
—ANONYMOUS

Paws for a minute and think about this . . .

The first mission of all new dog parents is to teach their pup not to go to the bathroom in the house. Some people take a hit-or-miss approach, giving their new dog free access to the outdoors by leaving a back door open or relying on a dog door.

Those who live in apartments often try the "pooping on paper" method, covering every inch of a room with newspapers. Then there are the owners who vaguely remember from past experience that crating a dog is the only way to housebreak it. So they crate their dog, not fully understanding why they are doing it, and not achieving their goal, either.

To take the guesswork out of understanding your dog's pooping pattern, I have devised an easy schedule for you to follow. This daily schedule teaches your pup to anticipate when he will be led outside to relieve himself. It also allows you the freedom to go about your day knowing there won't be a surprise for you to clean up after work, since your dog's needs have been met.

PUPPY PARENT GUILT

Most dog parents have to work and, therefore, they suffer tremen-
dous guilt about leaving their dog alone all day. Guilt leads them
to make excuses for their dog's not being housebroken. The schedule should help diminish those guilty feelings. Even if you work at
home, a schedule will give you the confidence that your pup is on
his way to becoming trustworthy.

With rescued adult dogs, it is also helpful to set up a schedule,
since many were kept in cages and had to relieve themselves in the
area in which they were kept. You should always reestablish
housebreaking for these dogs. Keeping to a schedule also helps a
new pooch become familiar with your daily patterns.

Any breed of dog can be housebroken, even the small ones. It
is a up to you to guide the dog. I have found that the biggest challenge in teaching people housebreaking techniques has always
been owner—not dog—resistance. Dogs are always eager to follow
their master's lead, provided the master acts with confidence and
offers encouragement. Owners, on the other hand, balk at simple
gating and crating techniques, which are key to training the dog to
hold the urge to eliminate.

People usually feel guilt about the wrong issues when it comes
to their dogs. Everyone feels terrible about leaving his or her dog
home alone for long periods of time. Even if you work at home,
time always seems better spent doing other things than attending
to your new pup's pooping pattern.

**Chew on this:** This feeling of guilt comes from not knowing
your dog's needs. The feeling is especially prevalent in people who
live in apartments and who own small-breed dogs. However, no
matter what size of dog you own, your pup can and should learn
to be housebroken. Oftentimes the people who feel the most guilt
about leaving their pooch alone all day are the same people who
don't exercise their dogs for weeks. I always tell people, if you
really feel bad about leaving your dog gated, then by all means
make time to exercise your dog in a park for an hour every morning. Believe me, your guilt will go away.

It is not a bad thing to teach your dog to hold the urge to go to
the bathroom. You wouldn't want a five-year old child in diapers
would you? Do your dog the favor of helping him learn control.

People Training

Understanding your pup's basic needs will give you a better perspective on how to incorporate his requirements into your daily routine. The following list is not meant to be patronizing. The most intelligent people complicate the basics of housebreaking by making a simple process complex. Your dog's general needs are to eat, play, poop, pee, chew, exercise, and, last but not least, learn from you.

The key to getting your dog not to pee in the house is to fit your dog's needs into your daily routine.

PEEING AND POOPING IN YOUR HOUSE

Housebreaking your dog is not only about getting your dog to go to the bathroom outside. It teaches your puppy to hold its urge to go until you take it outside. This is the part of housebreaking that must happen in stages. For example, an eight-week-old puppy is not mature enough physically to resist the urge to eliminate for eight hours while inside the house.

To have a fully housebroken dog also means that you trust your pet will not go to the bathroom while in your house or apartment. I often hear people say, "My dog is *pretty* well housebroken." They do not realize that housebreaking means learning to hold the urge to eliminate in all areas of the house and knowing the route outside. This takes time, over several developmental stages, like the potty-training process every child undergoes.

It is very common, however, to *sort* of housebreak your dog and be fooled. Actors Marg Helgenberger (*China Beach*) and her husband Alan Rosenberg (*Cybill*) did what many new dog owners do: they let their dog roam in and out of the house throughout the day. With the back door to the yard left wide open, Momo, a very sweet two-year-old pit bull–Lab mix, was able to go to the bathroom during the day at his leisure. Marg and Alan thought, "Great, that was easy. He is housebroken." Wrong. Marg began to discover pee stains on her favorite rug in the living room. Since she did not catch Momo peeing, she didn't want to scold him. A week later she discovered yet another "accident" in a different room of the house.

That was the last straw. Marg called me. "I don't get it," she said. "Momo was housebroken and now he is having lots of mistakes in the house. He's not a puppy anymore. What do I do?"

The problem was that Momo was never housebroken in the first place. Leaving a back door open and allowing your pup to float in and out of the house never teaches him to hold the urge. Momo was peeing in the living room in the middle of the night. How was he to know he wasn't supposed to relieve himself in the living room? The back door was not open at night, and he had never been reprimanded for peeing inside.

It is common for dogs who have never been formally housebroken to have the occasional mistake. I taught Marg and Alan to apply the five steps of housebreaking and the problem was solved. *Remember, it is never too late to housebreak your dog.*

<u>Chew on this:</u> All dogs, like their owners, have to go to the bathroom. It is a function, not a behavior. *Where* they go to the bathroom becomes a behavior over time. Depending on your pup's age, getting him to pee outside is a *process*. The success of this process depends on your consistency and your dog's developmental stage.

People training

Here are five simple steps to make your life easier during the housebreaking stage of puppyhood. The key is to fit your dog's needs into your daily routine. This is how it is done:

1. Gate and crate your dog.
2. Formally take your dog "Outside" on a leash.
3. Use a potty schedule to learn when your pup goes to the bathroom.
4. Feed your dog at regular times.
5. Reprimand your dog properly.

Let's review each step in detail.

Step One: Gating Your Dog and Teaching Him to "Wait"

Begin by gating your dog. Choose an area in your house, such as the kitchen, and put all of your pooch's toys and chew bones in that area along with a dog crate. Don't forget the water! For the first several weeks, the door of the crate should be removed, allowing your dog to freely acclimate to the crate. The crate serves as his condo or little den within the gated area. To get your pup into the gated area, put him on a leash, say, "Let's go," and guide him into the gated space. (If you do not use a leash, you will be coaxing your puppy, which gives him an opportunity not to follow you.)

Once inside the gated area, guide your dog to sit by lifting up on the leash. Repeat "Sit" as you raise the leash, until he sits. Keep your voice nice. When the pup is seated, say "Wait," step backward, out of the puppy area and put up the gate, then take off the leash and training collar. "Wait" means hang out in the gated space, not stay in one position.

To get your dog out of the gated area, the same process applies. Lean over the gate and your dog will come forward to greet you. Put on the leash and tell your dog to "Sit," lifting the leash up. When your dog sits, say "Wait" and remove the gate. If your dog tries to bolt out of the area, say "No!" Give the leash three quick tugs while saying, "No! No! No!" Having your dog on a leash, in this instance, teaches him not to bolt through a doorway. It also teaches him to focus on you and have eye contact before you direct him out of the gated area.

Your dog will experience a lot of anxiety about getting out of the gated area if you do not put him on a leash. By putting him on a leash first, you reassure him that the next step will be to leave the area together. Once he sits and waits and you have removed the gate, get eye contact from your dog by drawing your hand up from his nose to your eyes and saying the release command, "O.K." Guide him through the doorway directly outside while saying the word "Outside," meaning go potty.

<u>Note:</u> For a very young pup, eight to sixteen weeks old, put newspaper down at one end of his gated area, allowing him to go potty on the paper if necessary. Clean up the soiled newspaper frequently. When your pup is four months old, take away all newspapers in the area *forever*.

If your pup is age four months or older, do not use newspaper in the gated area. It would be a mixed signal. It is time to go cold turkey and teach your pup not to pee indoors. After the age of four months your puppy can learn to hold the urge to eliminate for many hours. Besides, the dog will probably just rip up the paper because he is in the teething stage.

Chew on this: Using a leash to get your pup in and out of the gated area is the key. The leash prevents you from developing bad habits such as coaxing, begging, or chasing your dog into the gated area. When we use such behaviors we create misbehavior in our dogs. In other words, your pup will learn to dodge your chasing, ignore your coaxing, or bark at your begging. Using a leash to guide your pup is the way to go.

People Training

The pup's gated area is his playpen, where he can enjoy his chew bones and play when you are preoccupied with other things. He can have free time with you in the house when you know that he has relieved himself outside.

Gating your dog also teaches him how to hang out in his own space, whether you are at home or not. After a couple of weeks, your pup will get used to being gated for longer periods of time, as you gradually extend his time in the gated area. Remember, the goal is that one day your dog will have the entire house as his area. After several weeks of acclimating your dog to a gated area, which is the crucial first step, it is time to use the crate as well.

Crating Is a Phase of Step One

The crate is a useful, portable tool for housebreaking. Crating allows you to move your dog's den to different areas in your home, such as your bedroom at night, to teach your pup to hold the urge to go the bathroom in each location. (Review the steps of crating in Chapter 5, "Creating Positive Boundaries.") Before crating, be sure to take your pup on a nice walk and play with him. Then give him a chew bone if he will be crated for a couple of hours. Crate your dog for just an hour or two a day, in addition to gating him for a few hours in the house. You can vary the length of time and the location of crating, but you should always guide your dog in and out of the crate on a leash, and take him directly outside when time's up. Taking shortcuts when formally teaching your dog where to go to the bathroom is how problems begin.

PAW PRINT: The idea of dogs as indoor pets didn't arise until the early nineteenth century, brought about by society when the urban middle class was born.

Step Two: Formally Taking Your Dog "Outside" on a Leash

Most new dog parents expect their dog to signal to them that he has to go to the bathroom, rather than themselves initiating "Outside" on a leash four or five times a day. Your dog needs to learn a pattern of when to go to the bathroom, based on *your* daily routine, not the other way around.

<u>*Chew on this:*</u> Consistency is very important for your dog during this step, and that's where most people mess up. They get lazy and do not put the dog on the leash while guiding him outside, or they just open the back door and let the dog take care of business on his own, never knowing if he has actually gone to the bathroom.

People Training

From the crate or gated area, put your dog on a leash and formally guide him outside, saying "Outside" as you go. A potty trip outside should only be a two- or three-minute break, not an exercise walk. It is to teach your pup to pee and poop on command. Take him to the same spot "Outside." People who live in a house with a backyard can create a gravel area and teach their pup to use it. This will make cleanup easier and keep your grass from being ruined. Just make sure that the area you create is big enough for your dog to be able to walk back and forth as he chooses a spot to relieve himself.

By initiating "Outside" on a leash four or five times a day, you can get your dog to go to the bathroom on command. Remember, exercise walks should be considered separate outings.

Step Three: Using a Potty Schedule to Learn When Your Pup Regularly Goes to the Bathroom

You're probably thinking, "You're kidding me, right? I don't have time to keep a potty schedule. How hard can taking my dog outside once in a while be?" Once you learn how often and when your dog eliminates, you can gauge if your dog's needs are being met by your daily routine. The ritual of going "Outside" regularly teaches your dog to poop and pee on command eventually, which is quite a huge time-saver in the long run.

<u>*Chew on this:*</u> I have created a potty schedule to help take the guesswork out of when your dog has to go to the bathroom. As silly as this sounds, it is helpful to housebreak your dog by fitting his elimination pattern into your daily routine.

People Training

The form below shows times of the day on the left-hand side and days of the week across the top of the page. To chart your dog's pattern of elimination, just fill in the times he goes "Outside" or has an accident. Write #1 for pee, #2 for poop, #3 for both, and * (an asterisk) for an accident, each day at the time your puppy goes potty.

After one week of using the schedule, you should begin to see a pattern to your dog's activities. Young puppies are more erratic, so you'll need to fill out the chart for several weeks and continue monitoring your pup's progress through different stages of development. Over a period of a month you should see that your dog eliminates at approximately the same times every day. Even if he is an older dog that you rescued from a shelter, follow the five steps of housebreaking and implement the potty schedule for up to a month. The potty schedule should be used until you feel that your pup or dog is regularly going to the bathroom on command and not having any accidents for a while.

 PAW PRINT: When a dog marks over another dog's scent, it leaves a sort of personal identification tag, including its gender, age, and health, thereby helping establish the dog's territory.

POTTY SCHEDULE
Week #_____

	SAT.	SUN.	MON.	TUES.	WED.	THUR.	FRI.
6:00							
7:00							
8:00							
9:00							
10:00							
11:00							
12:00							
1:00							
2:00							
3:00							
4:00							
5:00							
6:00							
7:00							
8:00							
9:00							
10:00							
11:00							
12:00							
1:00AM-6:00AM							

1 = pee   2 = poop   3 = both   * = accident

Step Four: Timed Feeding

There are two schools of thought on feeding. One advocates free feeding, which means leaving food out for your puppy at all times. The problem with free feeding is that if your puppy eats at odd times of the day, he will go to the bathroom at irregular times and it will be difficult to keep an accurate potty schedule. Also, this method often creates a finicky appetite over time.

The other method is timed feeding, which means that you set out your pup's food at regularly scheduled times for twenty minutes only. If he doesn't finish his food, it's "Sorry, Charlie" until the next feeding. This method teaches your pup to eat a meal at the time you serve it. Timed feedings help keep your dog's elimination on schedule, too.

I prefer timed feeding for my dogs because of my hectic lifestyle. It assures me that their nutritional needs are being met and they'll be ready to poop on schedule.

<u>*Chew on this:*</u> According to the timed feeding method, the feeding schedule of your dog depends on its age. Here is a suggested timetable:

- *8 weeks–3½ months:* feed three times a day or free feed
- *4 months–1 year:* feed twice a day
- *1 year and up:* feed once a day

<u>Note:</u> Some veterinarians recommend twice-a-day feeding for adult dogs as well as puppies.

Dogs should be fed according to their weight. Ask your veterinarian how much to feed your breed of dog.

People Training

Many owners unintentionally end up overfeeding their adult dogs. Whether to feed your adult dog once or twice a day is a personal choice, but it should suit your daily schedule and lifestyle. I have always fed my adult dogs once a day, along with giving them a few hard dog biscuits for breakfast and teeth cleaning. They have done just fine. But here's some food for thought: many adult dogs, as they get older, do not often get the required exercise for their breed. Hence they get fat. Therefore, know that your dog's best treat of all is a walk.

Step Five: Reprimanding Your Dog in a Way That Makes Sense to Him

Most dogs get into trouble when you're not around. They chew things you value or they go to the bathroom where they shouldn't. Both of these acts are normal functions of a dog: to chew and to poop and pee. Where they go to the bathroom and what they chew may become bad behaviors over time. You do not have to catch your dog in the act of doing something wrong in order to reprimand him. Having to catch your dog in the act can become an exhausting part-time job.

If your dog knew not to pee on the carpet, he simply wouldn't do it. People think that their dog knows exactly what he has done wrong. The hardest thing for people to realize is that dogs do not reason. It is up to you, the owner, to ensure that your dog learns to go potty outside.

<u>**Chew on this:**</u> Along with showing your dog what he has done wrong, it is equally important to show your dog how to please you.

People Training

The only way to reprimand your dog so that the message is clear to him is to guide him on a leash. If you do not use a leash and merely scold him, your dog will react to your stern voice inflection, but not understand why you are mad. He needs to associate the smell of the urine on the carpet with your displeasure.

Using a leash, guide your dog to the mistake. If you walk toward your pup in an angry way, he will run away. Wouldn't you? Instead, you should be smarter than your dog. Crouch down and in a happy voice call your dog to you, away from the mistake. Put him on the leash and then guide him over to his error. In a stern voice say "No!" and put your dog's nose near the spot—*not* in it. Repeat "No!" several times and then whisk him outside, saying the word "Outside" to indicate where you want him to go to the bathroom. Take a paper towel dabbed in the urine outside with you. Put it on the ground, end the reprimand by saying "O.K. Outside," and then praise him: "Good dog!"

*   *   *

The following recaps the process of how to reprimand your dog. Remember, all commands and reprimands must have a beginning, a middle, and an end.

The Beginning

- Get the leash.

- Use reverse psychology: get your pup to come to you by crouching down and calling him in a happy voice.

- Put the leash on your pooch and guide him over to his mistake, whether it's an accident (soiling the carpet) or something valuable that he has chewed.

The Middle

- Put your pup's nose near it, not in it, and say, "NO! NO! NO!" in a firm voice. Whether it's defecation or a gnawed shoe—what you are saying "No" to is the scent of urine on the carpet or the scent of saliva on your shoe.

The End

- Take him outside on the leash. Say "Outside" in a happy voice. Take the scent of the mistake with you (e.g., his urine on a paper towel). Put it on the ground. Say "O.K. Outside. Good dog!" This signals to your pup how to please you and says that the reprimand is formally over. Take off the leash and have fun. In the case of the chewed item, offer your dog a chew bone after the reprimand and then say "O.K."

Truth-or-Tail Pup Quiz

Test your knowledge and try to match the following notions about how to reprimand a dog. Do you identify with the habits of the following breeds of dog owners? Do any of the scenarios sound familiar to you? Are they Truths or Tails?

1) Human habits of the *It's O.K. Owner*   Truth or Tail?
   Catching the dog in the act of doing something
   wrong is the only time you can reprimand him.

2) Human habits of the *Talker*   Truth or Tail?
   A dog knows exactly what he has done wrong.
   When you say, "What did you do?" his ears go
   back and he runs out of the room.

3) Human habits of the *Control Freak*   Truth or Tail?
   When you punish a dog, you need to put him
   outside and let him think about what he did
   wrong.

4) Human habits of the *Smacker*   Truth or Tail?
   When a dog does something wrong you should
   try to catch him and then hit him on the nose
   with a rolled newspaper.

ANSWERS TO THE TRUTH-OR-TAIL PUP QUIZ

1) Chew on this tail: The answer is No! You do not have to catch your dog in the act of doing something wrong. What you are saying "No!" to is not the act of going to the bathroom, but rather *where* the dog went to the bathroom. What your dog needs to associate with the word "No!" is the scent of urine or poop on the floor or carpet. That is what you are reprimanding him for.

2) Chew on this tail: If dogs could reason and if they knew exactly what they did wrong, then my dog could come over and train your dog and we could go out and have a cafè latte. All dogs want to please you; they just don't know how. If your dog really knew not to relieve himself in the house, he simply wouldn't do it.

Dogs respond to voice inflection and body language. So if you walk into the house and yell "What did you do?" at your dog, he will appear to know that you are mad, but he won't know why. He is nervous because you sound mad.

3) Chew on this tail: If your dog is thinking about what he has done wrong because he is confined to the backyard as a form of punishment, I would like to hire him to balance my checkbook. Once he is through chasing those squirrels in the backyard, of course.

4) Chew on this tail: NEVER, EVER CHASE OR HIT YOUR DOG. If you want that much exercise, you should go to the gym. Chasing him and dragging him over to his mistake only indicates to your dog that you are mad. It doesn't show him what he has done wrong.

Aggression only breeds aggression, it does not solve the problem. Hitting your dog will only create more problems. Dominant dogs may become aggressive toward you, and submissive dogs may begin to spot pee because they become so distressed by your anger. No matter what your dog has done wrong, you need to ask yourself if you have met all of your dog's needs. Then, through training, not through hitting, show your dog how to please you.

If you answered "truth" to any of the four quiz questions, reread step five on how to reprimand your dog. These four common habits are how human behavior can cause misbehavior in our dogs. Getting your dog not to pee in your house is a product of all five steps combined: gating, initiating "Outside" on a leash, using the potty schedule, timed feeding, and reprimanding your dog properly so that it makes sense to him. All of the housebreaking steps work together to show your dog how to please you.

Some people take shortcuts in housebreaking their puppies by incorporating a doggy door too soon.

DOGGY DOORS

If you have skipped a step and think your dog is housebroken because you have a dog door, you may be in for a surprise. Many people suffer from doggy-owner denial surrounding this house-breaking issue. I get calls saying "I thought my dog was house-broken, but he still has mistakes in the house occasionally. He is two years old and he mostly uses the dog door." Don't think that because you leave a door open or have a dog door your dog will automatically know to go outside, almost like a cat in a litter box. Wrong. No matter the age or size of your dog, proper training is crucial.

Some people think it's cruel to leave a dog without access to the outdoors for eight-hour periods. That's why the dog door was invented. My opinion is that it's hard to have your cake and eat it too. Doggy doors can create all sorts of bad behavioral problems, such as territorialism and excessive barking. This happens over time as your dog learns to bolt out the dog door to protect his property or bark at noises in the neighbor's yard. In addition, having a dog door never teaches your dog to control his urge to relieve himself.

I feel a dog door works if you have already formally potty-trained your dog, and when your dog has matured. Then you can have the benefits of both—the convenience of the dog door, and a trustworthy, housebroken dog. Waiting until your pup is house-broken and fully mature is the best idea if you want to install a dog door.

After many months of applying the five steps of housebreaking, you can incorporate a dog door. Take the time to teach your dog in a consistent manner. Using a leash, take your pup from the gated area, saying "Outside" while guiding your pup to the doggy door. Show your pup a treat and throw the treat through the dog door. Your puppy should bounce through the dog door after the treat. If he doesn't, lift the flap of the dog door and, if necessary, throw an additional treat through the opening. Your pup should follow after the treat with a little encouragement. Then open the door that has the dog door opening and meet your pup on the other side. Take the leash and guide your puppy to his toilet area in the backyard. Repeat this process every time you initiate "Outside" with your pup. Repetition of this process will bring success.

TAIL WAG: THE NORTON FAMILY

There is an art to teaching your pup how to use a dog door. This is what my clients the Peter Norton family, known for Norton Utilities computer software and their prominent art collection, had to learn. Their family dog Daisy, a Standard Poodle, needed to be taught not to redecorate the art work that graced their home with her own form of freestanding sculptures. Through formal training, Daisy learned how to hold her urge to go to the bathroom throughout the house and know the route outside, even from remote rooms that were not always used by the family. One of the goals for Daisy's training was to eventually incorporate a doggy door into her routine, so that she could become self-sufficient in her bathroom duties. This goal could be achieved only by teaching the family to follow the five steps of housebreaking. First came gating and crating Daisy for an hour or two at different times in different rooms of the large house. This exercise taught her to hold the urge to eliminate and, on leash, follow the route outside through a dog door. After several months of this routine, the goal was achieved and Daisy now has the run of the house—without a single accident. The Norton family learned that the art of applying the five steps of housebreaking was invaluable. Daisy remains priceless.

Adopted with a talent for creating smiles.

•

OWNER
Leila Kenzle, actress
PHOTOGRAPH BY JONATHAN EXLEY

Pedigree pup who is programmed to amuse.

•

OWNERS
Peter Norton family,
Norton Utilities computer software, art collectors
PHOTOGRAPH BY JONATHAN EXLEY

Famous for goosing guests at the door.

•

OWNERS
Marg Helgenberger, actress
Alan Rosenberg, actor
PHOTOGRAPH BY JONATHAN EXLEY

Picture perfect.
Lost on the freeway and found love.

•

OWNER
Jonathan Exley, photographer
PHOTOGRAPH BY JONATHAN EXLEY

• BABY GIRL • • MURPHY •

Doberman Mix   Spaniel Mix

Rescued from a trash dumpster and now
traveling with J.D. for life.

•

OWNER

J. D. Souther, songwriter

PHOTOGRAPH BY JONATHAN EXLEY

• BODHI • • MISS DAISY •
German Shepherd   Terrier Mix

Pawsing for a moment
with my kids.

•

OWNER
Inger Martens

PHOTOGRAPH BY JONATHAN EXLEY

Practice makes perfect!

Inger at age 4 training a
family friend's dog.

Ability to hit the high notes
along with his mama.

•

OWNER
LeAnn Rimes, singer
PHOTOGRAPH BY ROSS PELTON

Gnawing on Your Last Nerve

True friendship is never serene.
—MARQUISE DE SÉVIGNÉ

Paws for a minute and think about this . . .

High on the Top 10 list of what annoys all new puppy parents is a combo of biting, chewing, gnawing, and nipping. Whatever you want to call it, when your little angel begins to turn into Jaws it's shocking, not to mention irritating.

Do you reprimand this behavior or do you try to tolerate it? A pup's teething stage can be completely misunderstood by new dog parents and therefore handled incorrectly. Most people try to discipline their pup for his need to chew, equating the teething stage to obnoxious, out-of-control behavior.

In fact, a puppy's need to chew is a matter of function, not behavior. What your dog chooses to chew on, such as your furniture, becomes a behavior over time.

Between the ages of three and a half months and five months, all of your pup's teeth will loosen and fall out and new ones will grow in. By the time your dog is six months old, he will have all-new adult teeth. Teaching your pooch what he can and cannot chew on becomes your job. Some people have battle wounds and it's hard not to take this puppy stage personally. The main thing to realize is that *you* are the main student, not your dog. So what do you do?

NIPPING

Do you have teeth marks on your arm from your pup's nipping? Many people feel that puppy biting is a behavior that needs to be disciplined. Do you reprimand nipping?

<u>Chew on this:</u> When a young puppy nips he is often responding to the movement of your hand waving in front of his face as you try to pat him. This presents a catch-22. Show your pup affection and your hand becomes a moving target. Puppies find any movement stimulating. When you walk by, a pup might nip at your leg in sport. He would wrestle with another pup the same way. Remember, puppies play with each other by biting and nipping. So how do you cope?

People Training

Do not try to reprimand this nipping with a constant chorus of "No!" You can't teach a five-month-old puppy to be a seven-year-old dog. Some dogs teethe worse than others. Some pups are in pain because large adult teeth are trying to poke through sore gums. Therefore your pooch has a license to be Jaws.

If your pup gets into a nipping-and-biting mood, you need to set a precedent by giving him a pig's ear or some other permissible object to chew instead of your hand. If that doesn't do the trick, then guide the play by moving the chew toy around. He will get stimulated by the movement of the toy rather than your hand and eventually get tired. As a last resort, you could vigorously exercise him and then gate him with a new pig's ear, not as a punishment but rather as an alternative.

When you are not free to supervise your human baby, you put him or her in a playpen with toys. The same goes for a young, teething puppy. When new puppy parents do not provide chew toys appropriate for the dog's age and give their young pups too much freedom, basic functions, such as chewing, become frustrating behaviors.

CHEWING

The need to chew itself is a natural need or a function for a dog, and especially for a puppy. Now that you know this, the million-dollar question becomes, how are you supposed to survive this Jaws phase of puppydom and end up with a well-behaved dog? Some dogs in their teenage stage have high anxiety combined with a voracious need to chew. This combination can lead to major destruction. If a dog is repeatedly allowed to do an action, such as chew on your furniture, it will become a bad behavior over time.

Suppose you do fail to catch your dog in the act of destroying your sofa. First, your adolescent puppy should not be loose in the house when you are not at home or not able to spend quality time with him. Until your dog is trained and trustworthy (which takes time), he should be gated with chew bones during those times that you can't focus on him. Second, the key to not feeling guilty about this gating routine is to make sure all of your dog's exercise and bathroom needs are met before you gate him for that hour. We all need to have a routine to organize our life, and a schedule will help promote positive behaviors rather than let negative ones like chewing furniture happen. To avoid further destruction you also need to reexamine your puppy's chew toys when he turns four or five months old. You may feel that your dog has plenty to play with; however, his chewing needs have escalated dramatically. The toys that were once appropriate don't cut the mustard anymore for your teenage pup. Chew bones, hooves, and pig's ears should not be regarded as treats or rewards; they are a necessity. Make sure you have plenty of them on the floor at all times during this stage. This will prevent a dog from chewing on your furniture, which can become a destructive, anxiety-ridden habit, much like smoking is for some humans. Without the proper rules and chew items, a dog will regard your furniture as the next best thing.

**Chew on this:** Lack of supervision, exercise, and proper chew bones can contribute to the need to chew becoming a bad behavior, resulting in destruction of your property. Puppy-proofing your house and exercising your dog a lot are your best defenses against this potential problem.

People Training

A common complaint is that after the owner has spent a lot of money on dog toys the destruction still happens. As a trainer, before I look at the damaged rug, I first check to see how many chew bones are on the floor. I ask whether the dog has plenty of chew bones available. The response is always an emphatic "Yes." As I look around, there are never any chew bones in sight. Toys, yes. Chew bones, like chewy rolls, pig's ears, or rawhide, no. When I say "I don't see any," the reply is that the pup takes them outside or they always seem to disappear.

My suggestion for everyone who relates to this scenario is to make sure when you are with your pup during free time that there are plenty of new things to chew. If you cannot keep an eye on your pup, then exercise him and gate him for a short time with a chew bone. Remember, it is your job to make sure the chew bones are in front of your puppy to chew.

Bonafide Facts about Chewing

• Believe it or not, you need to teach your pup to chew on that five-dollar bone you just bought him.

• Leaving your shoes lying around the house and not gating a rambunctious pup when you are preoccupied can lead to costly mishaps.

• Your dog has not chewed up your favorite rug just to get even with you for going to the movies. The destruction is the result of not puppy-proofing your house enough. Your pup simply does not know what's off-limits.

• Teach your dog not to become territorial over his bones. Show him not to become possessive over his bones by occasionally holding one for a few minutes while he chews on it.

• Reprimand your dog in the correct way for chewing things that are yours.

Gnawing on Your Last Nerve: How to Reprimand Your Dog the Right Way

Your dog has just chewed on the leg of your favorite table. Do you walk into the room and (*a*) scream "No!" at your dog, convinced that he knows exactly what he has done wrong; (*b*) blame the whole incident on your spouse for wanting to go out to dinner in the first place; or (*c*) do nothing because you didn't catch your dog in the act of chewing the table leg. The correct answer is (*d*) none of the above.

<u>**Chew on this:**</u> You do not have to catch your dog chewing something in order to reprimand him. You can reprimand your dog after the fact. If you come home and discover a chewed item and then do not reprimand your dog you are giving him a mixed signal. You must clearly show him that chewing your shoes is not O.K. Oh, you may be mad all right, but your dog truly does not understand what he has done wrong. Remember, chewing is a function of dogs. They have to chew.

The scent of the item your dog has chewed is what you want to clearly identify as a negative to your dog. Then you want to identify for him the scent of the item he is allowed to chew. Keep reading and find out how.

People Training

Reprimand your dog for chewing the wrong thing as follows:
Calmly put your dog on a leash and walk him over to the item he has chewed. The leash is an important tool. It allows you to take him to his mistake, rather than pull him by his collar. Put his nose near the item so he can smell what he has chewed. Then in a low, stern voice say "NO! NO! NO!" This communicates to him that his saliva on the item he has chewed is a "No." Then guide him on leash over to his rawhide bone or pig's ear and say "O.K." in a happy voice. This way the reprimand has a beginning, middle, and end. The ending shows him what is okay to chew. Remember, you are not saying "No" to the act of chewing, because all dogs need to chew. In terms of the reprimand, you are simply saying "No" to *what* your dog has chewed and providing an alternative.

Puppy-proof your home as much as possible during the teething stage. Do not leave shoes, socks, and other items around for your pup to destroy.

What to Buy Your Pup at What Age

• *Best teething toys for a three- to four-and-a-half-month-old puppy:* Most popular are pig's ears, stuffed squeaky toys, and hard rubber balls.

<u>*Chew on this:*</u> The big attraction for this age group are the squeaky toys or anything that rolls. Teething is in its beginning stage and any toy is of interest.

People Training
Pig's ears are more digestible and better for teething than plastic and stuffed toys. If your puppy begins to destroy a stuffed squeaky toy, take it away and keep the pig's ears coming. It means your pup's teething is painful and he needs to get those teeth loose.

• *Best teething bones for four to six months of age on up through adulthood:* Pig's ears, chewy rolls, carrot bones, rawhide, and hooves.

<u>*Chew on this:*</u> A dog's general need to chew lasts until the age of two to three years and then tapers off to an occasional chewing hobby. Think of chewing as a necessity for your dog. It helps his puppy teeth fall out and pacifies him when you are away or not in the mood to play.

People Training
The need to chew becomes acute because your puppy needs to loosen all of his teeth so they can fall out. Sometimes the baby teeth do not fall out before the new teeth start to grow in; this increases the chewing desire. It's a good idea to look into your pup's mouth occasionally to see what's going on with his teeth.

In addition to keeping a lot of chew things on the floor for your dog, exercise is also important. Exercise can be a big help in fighting destructive chewing. If you plan to be out for the evening, give your dog a good run a few hours before you leave. This will leave your dog tired and content to hang out and chew his bone while you are away.

 PAW PRINT: A 40-pound dog can chomp down with a force of approximately 350 pounds of pressure.

Bone to Pick: the Rawhide Controversy

Is rawhide good for your dog? Many people are confused about giving their dog rawhide as a chew bone. Some dog parents believe it is hard to digest. Others swear by it. What's the deal about rawhide?

<u>**Chew on this:**</u> As mentioned earlier, rawhide comes from the hide of a cow or buffalo. These hides are cut up and formed into shapes in different sizes, and dogs love them. Are they good for your dog? Every dog is different. Some have delicate stomachs and others do not. Some dogs have stomach ailments and cannot digest the rawhide as easily. My recommendation is to check with your vet.

Rawhide is sold in most pet stores. From puppyhood through adulthood, dogs need to chew, a lot. If you don't provide them with the proper outlet for this need, they may become doggy delinquents.

People Training

Often a puppy's need to chew is so acute that if you do not provide satisfying chews, the puppy ends up eating his plastic toys and your furniture. I would rather my dog chewed on rawhide than on my couch or favorite pillow. However, there are rawhide issues to consider, so keep reading.

The Dos and Don'ts of Rawhide

✓ DO

• Check with your vet. Some puppies and adult dogs have a problem digesting rawhide.

• Some types of rawhide are safer than others. The best is pressed rawhide. It has many layers that make it heavier, denser, and longer-lasting. Look for the rawhide with a natural light brown color.

• Replace rawhide frequently. Throw away pieces that get too small. It may seem costly, but it could save your dog from choking.

• Look into alternatives to rawhide, such as chewy rolls, carrot bones, and hooves. You may need to experiment to find what works for your dog and your situation.

✗ DON'T

• Do not buy rawhide in pieces that are too small for your puppy. They can get caught in his throat and choke him. Make sure the pieces are the appropriate size for your breed of puppy.

• If you have two dogs of different sizes, gate them separately so that the larger dog doesn't choke on the smaller dog's rawhide bone.

DOGGEDLY CHALLENGED?

The teenage stage can be the most trying of all for some dog parents. Are you experiencing any of the following behavioral responses?

• Stubbornness
• Erratic behavior
• Inexplicable aggression
• Unwillingness to cooperate
• A propensity to be easily distracted

If you think I'm talking about your dog, think again. I'm talking about you! What I'm describing is the type of dog owner who is prone to find fault with training techniques. Such owners think their dog is too stubborn or stupid to learn. The listed behavioral responses begin to apply to the owner's behavior, not the dog's.

Many first-time dog owners are doggedly challenged. They feel as though their dog is purposely destroying things to get back at them for going to work. You may have a family member or a spouse who fits into this category.

The doggedly challenged often complain that their puppy exhibits behavioral problems, not realizing they may not be meeting the dog's needs—for example, not giving the dog either enough exercise or proper chew bones.

Your puppy's chewing and exercise needs can change within a few months as he matures from toddler to adolescent. If you don't keep up with the changes by buying more chew bones and providing enough exercise, the result could be occasional destruction. What the owner sees as stubbornness or random acts of destruction on the part of his new pup is simply evidence of the growing pains of puppyhood, or of the owner's inconsistency.

Do not give your dog items like old shoes to chew. Your dog does not know the difference between new and old. This inconsistency, or laziness, just confuses your dog. It is up to you to show your dog what to chew.

Keep in mind that chewing is simply a stage of development, not bad behavior directed at you. Your puppy may begin to need more exercise and stimulation before being gated or left alone while you are at work.

There are sprays available that deter puppies from chewing on things that they shouldn't; these help to protect furniture. In addition to puppy-proofing in your home, you need to provide more training. If anything, this is the most crucial time to keep the training going. Hang in there; it does get easier. Give your dog the benefit of the doubt, and stick with the process of training. Sometimes the only way to get around something is to go through it.

TAIL WAG:
MARG HELGENBERGER AND ALAN ROSENBERG

Many behavioral issues can be reduced by exercise. Life can be a walk on a beach, but sometimes our daily schedule doesn't allow it to be quite that blissful. Emmy award–winning actress Marg Helgenberger and actor Alan Rosenberg both have busy schedules and often don't have the time to take their dog on long walks. Momo is a supersweet pit bull–Lab mix who dispels any stigma attached to his Staffordshire bull terrier—a.k.a. pit bull—heritage. With the proper training and socialization, Momo is a perfect wide receiver for the couple's seven-year-old son, Hughy.

The problem was that playing with Momo required equipment just short of a helmet for Hughy. The family needed to learn how to curb Momo's exuberance yet still meet his need to play. Momo would often grab one of Hughy's toys and take off, instigating a game of chase. If he wasn't chased, the toy was quickly destroyed. Teaching the family how to play fetch with Momo was a big help in meeting his exercise needs. A twenty-minute game of fetch allowed both Hughy and Momo to remain star athletes. Time out became Momo's time to chew his bone.

How to Play Fetch: Creating the Ball-A-Holic

For dogs with a high energy level and prey drive, playing fetch is a great form of exercise. Many dog owners complain that their pooch will go after the ball but will not always bring it back. The trick is to introduce the game of fetch with a little structure. Most people use methods of begging, pleading, coaxing, and sometimes chasing, trying to get their pup to bring the ball back. This form of cheerleading quickly turns into complaining when the dog just runs away with the ball and the game of fetch becomes touch football. Sound familiar?

People Training

You need to use anticipation as the incentive. Have a special ball that you use for the game of fetch only. Keep this ball in a drawer and take it out just for fetch. When introducing the game, ask your dog to sit, while you hold the ball in your hand. Then say "O.K." and throw the ball. As your pup gets the ball, crouch down and clap your hands, praising your pup. As he runs toward you, take a treat out of your back pocket. Suddenly stand up from the crouching position. Then guide your dog into a "Sit" while holding the treat. He will spit out the ball in exchange for the treat. Give him the treat, pick up the ball, and begin again.

The trick is to throw the ball just twice the first time you introduce the game of fetch. Then put the ball away, until another day. The next time you play fetch, repeat the same process, increasing to three throws and so on. In this way the game of fetch slowly becomes a fun ritual for you and your pup, with a win-win score.

To correct bad habits, you might adjust the game of fetch by using reverse psychology and foresight. If your dog dodges you, reverse the game and make him chase you a few feet; next, crouch down suddenly, and then praise him as he moves toward you. The key is to stand up as he comes running toward you, guiding him into a "Sit" using the treat. Being smarter than your dog should enable you to undo any bad habits that may have been created in the past.

To have a well-behaved dog in your house requires bonding, training, and sufficient exercise. Now that you have met some of your pup's basic needs, let's get to the training.

Unleashing the Driver in You

If you think education is expensive, try ignorance.
—DEREK BOK

Do you get dragged down the street on your daily walk? Does your dog have selective hearing and only listen to you when you have a treat in your hand? "My dog only comes to me when he wants a treat." Sound familiar?

Primarily, people ask me to train their dogs to control bad behavior. Training is not about trying to control your dog's bad behavior. It's about achieving focus. When your dog pays attention to you despite distractions and is intent on doing what you ask, that's focus.

Many people feel that their dogs are driving them down the street or just plain driving them crazy. So how do you get a dog's attention without constantly having to honk your horn? There should be no discipline involved in training your dog. Structure and consistency, yes. Yelling random instructions, no. It is up to you to make the process pleasant.

My client Lee, a thirty-two-year-old lawyer, owner of a Labrador-mix named Sonny, voiced the sentiments of many of my clients. "My dog will obey most commands for a treat, but when I call him, he just ignores me," Lee complained. Using treats to train your dog can give both you and your dog whiplash, or at least a mixed signal. Many owners unintentionally teach their dog to disobey, and then try to control the dog's bad behavior. Now I probably just gave *you* whiplash.

As I told Lee, training your dog to behave is similar to driving a car. There are basics in dog training, just as there are in driving. The basic commands for your dog are "Heel," "Sit," "Stay," "Wait," "Down," and "Come." Lee could relate much more to the process of driving a car than to a boot camp philosophy of dog training. He couldn't wait to learn how to teach his dog to cruise down the street and enjoy the scenery.

Speeding through the process of dog training is the first mistake that most people make. Some of us use bribery as a training method, taunting our dogs with treats while repeating words like "Sit" or "Stay," hoping the dog will catch on. Of course, the dog will eventually sit down out of anticipation of the treat, not because of the word "Sit." This method of training is equivalent to going to a foreign country and miming your destination to a taxi driver, while waving a hundred-dollar bill under his nose. The taxi driver will take your money and may get you were you want to go, in a roundabout way, but a clear understanding of the route was never reached. The same goes for your dog if you attempt to train him solely with treats. Give your dog all the treats and praise in the world, just don't expect treats to teach him the rules of the road.

ARE YOU THE DRIVER?

The main issue in training your dog is establishing who's the driver. You may be smiling and thinking, "Yeah, right. My dog drives me down the street, pulling and panting." But your dog is looking to you for guidance. When you wait to see what your dog is going to do in a situation, it gives him a wrong signal. It says he leads.

Your dog's temperament is just like a driver's disposition. Some people are assertive drivers and blow stoplights. Others are overly cautious and cause an accident out of fear. Dogs are similar. No matter what the breed, some dogs are born dominant and pull on a leash; some are submissive and lag behind as they walk. The tools that put you in the driver's seat are the leash and training collar.

Leash and Training Collar

Most people misunderstand the function of the training collar, or choke chain. They use it as if it were the brake on a car. It is not the brake, but functions as the blinker, or turn indicator. You need to indicate what you want from your dog by using the training collar and leash, giving lots of quick snaps or tugs, and reassuring your dog by directing him with a command. That is the way he'll know he is doing a good job.

Make sure your dog walks on *your left side* when you practice the "Heel" command, so that the training collar can tighten and quickly release with a quick snap of the leash. The fast tug or snap of the leash causes the training collar to make a slight jingle, which tells your dog to focus on a verbal command. It does not hurt the dog. Pulling, panting, and dragging you on a leash while wearing a regular nylon collar does. Believe it or not, pleasing you is important to your dog. The combination of leash, training collar, and a pleasant voice command clearly directs your pup to do what you want. Don't worry, the collar will release if you put it on properly and use a fast snap (pull and release) on the leash. (Review Chapter 4, "Bare-Bones Basics.") Remember, the leash and training collar will get your dog's attention. Your pleasant verbal command and praise are your dog's reward for doing a great job.

The training collar is not the brake on the dog. It functions more like the blinker, or turn indicator.

Learning to Drive Your Dog Down the Street

When we drive a car we have boundaries, such as roads and traffic lights. We know that when the light turns red we must stop and that green means go. The leash and training collar act as similar devices, indicators that tell your dog what you want him to do next.

For example, when walking your pooch, signal for him to stop by lifting up on the leash as you stop and say "Sit."

The leash and training collar act as indicators for your dog, telling him what you want him to do next, much like traffic lights for a driver. The main issue in dog training is establishing who drives.

A leash is not a long rope that you attach to your dog's collar so he won't run away. It may sound strange, but the leash operates like the wheel of the car. The leash is your most important tool in gaining control and keeping your dog's attention. Too many people train their dog through verbal repetition, without the leash. This is a bad habit that actually teaches your dog to eventually ignore you. Using the leash when teaching a command in your home allows you to guide your dog as you would drive a car down the street. It also creates trust and eye contact. All of this develops focus, which is key to communicating with your dog.

The leash is your most important tool in gaining your dog's focus.

Since dogs are pack animals, they like to follow the leader. If you don't instinctively take the wheel, they will. Your dog will think, "O.K., if you're not going to drive, I will," and pull you down the street. That's where the problems begin.

Rules of the Road: The Basic Commands of Obedience

1.   "Heel" or "Let's go" means walk on my left and at my heel.

2.   "Sit" means sit, not stay.

3.   "Stay" means do not move. (Not sort of, not kind of. Do not move.)

4.   "Down" means lie down. (Not do not jump on me, not get off the couch.)

5. "Come" means come to me and sit and wait for a release command.

6. "O.K." is the release command and means the command is over.

O.K. WHAT?

Every command should have a beginning, middle, and end. The word "O.K." signals your dog that a command (like "Sit" and "Stay") is over. A key part of the "O.K." command is to draw your dog's attention up to your eyes. Lead your dog to look at your eyes by using your hand. Put your hand to your dog's nose and then slowly draw your hand up to your eyes. Your dog's eyes will follow your hand. Once your dog is looking at you, then in a happy voice say "O.K.," and have a party. There should be some degree of formality attached to the ending of a specific task that you are asking of your dog. Your dog should learn to anticipate an ending to the command. This will give him clarity.

In this chapter, I offer the basics of obedience. In Chapter 9 I will explain where to apply them in your life. If you feel as though your dog is driving you, the following analogies to basic obedience commands will help put you back in the driver's seat.

HEEL: START YOUR ENGINES AND PRESS THE GAS PEDAL!

The "Heel" command signals a forward motion, functioning as a gas pedal. The word "Heel" tells your dog to walk at your side. It is quite simple. The leash and training collar let you indicate to your pup how fast you want to walk and saying "Heel" reinforces the message.

Just as the steering wheel is on the left in a car, the dog should be on your left-hand side as you walk. Remember, if the leash acts as the steering wheel, then the training collar works as the blinker or turn indicator. To turn right or left, you signal to your dog through quick snaps or jerks of the leash in the direction you want to go.

The direction is further set by your body motion. If you want to turn right, then walk to the right. If your dog is pulling you, then turn and walk in the opposite direction, saying "Heel" in a nice voice. He will have no choice but to follow you. After all, you are the driver, and he is on a leash. To indicate a stop, pull up on the leash, saying "Sit."

The following is a review of the four steps to heeling your pup.

How to Teach Your Dog to "Heel"

1. Have your dog "Sit" next to you on *your left-hand side*. Hold the *leash in your right hand*, then say "Heel" in a happy voice and start walking.

2. Say "Heel" or "Let's go" and give frequent quick jerks or snaps of the leash, indicating how fast you want to go. Don't forget to tell your pup what a good job he's doing.

3. If your dog begins to pull on the leash, pivot quickly in the opposite direction and say "Heel" in a happy voice. Then resume walking.

4. To stop your dog, stop walking and pull up on the leash, saying "Sit" in a nice voice. If your dog doesn't sit right away, repeat the word "Sit" while simultaneously pulling up on the leash again, repeating until your dog obeys.

Dog owners need to gain confidence in using the leash and training collar. As in driving a car, practice makes perfect. Otherwise, your dog will be zooming down the sidewalk at a hundred miles an hour, with you in the backseat.

What Kind of Fuel Are You Using: A Pleasant Voice or a Treat?

Getting your pooch's attention on the street is challenging because there are many smells, dogs, and other distractions. Short of honking a horn, people try everything to get control—coaxing, begging, and, when all else fails, yelling. Many dog parents give in and bribe their dogs to listen. Your dog's motivation to listen to you should come from your pleasant voice and guidance with a leash, not a treat. Your voice and the leash create the eye contact and focus you want to experience.

If you feel that you are identifying with either the Control Freak breed of dog owner or the Coaxer on a walk, watch it! The goal is to communicate with your dog without having to coax him (by bribing with a treat) or control the situation (by trying to enforce the command with an overly stern voice). Keep a pleasant, confident voice and make it fun for both of you.

> **Your dog's motivation to listen to you should come from your pleasant voice and guidance with a leash, not a treat.**

 PAW PRINT: Rin Tin Tin went from being a starving puppy rescued from the trenches of World War I to earning $5 million in 25 movies.

STAY: A RED TRAFFIC LIGHT

The "Stay" command means *do not move*. It will function like a red traffic light to your dog, not a stop sign. Many dog parents misuse this command by shouting "Stay!" at their dog without using the leash. You should formally teach your dog the "Stay" command on a leash.

How to Teach Your Dog to Stay

1. Put the training collar and leash on your dog.

2. Position your dog next to you on your left-hand side, so the collar works properly.

3.   Lift up and then down with the leash, as you say "Sit." Repeat until your dog sits. Remember, be nice. You are not hurting your dog with the training collar.

4.   Once your dog sits, say "Stay" and take a few steps, backing away from your dog. If he moves, which he probably will, lean down and reach just above the clasp on the leash and tug on the leash three times, saying a firm, quick "No! No! No!" in a low voice. Then in a nice voice, repeat "Sit," pulling up on the leash again.

It is important that your voice remain nice as you apply a command. Once he sits, then repeat "Stay" and move a few feet away. Repeat "Stay" in a nice, calm voice, as though you know what you're doing. Your dog may look at you in anticipation, but don't worry about this. Keep your voice calm and reassure him by saying "Stay" once more. Try to accomplish walking one full circle around your dog, while repeating the "Stay" command, without the dog moving. Don't let go of the leash.

5.   Once you have accomplished this, return next to him so that he is on your left-hand side. Take your hand and almost touch his nose, then draw your hand up to your eyes, creating eye contact. End the command by saying "O.K." The word "O.K." should act as a formal ending to all commands. It teaches your dog to anticipate a release.

Keep in mind that your dog is learning this for the first time. Be patient.

DOWN: PARKING THE CAR

The "Down" command means to lie down. You are indicating to your dog that he should relax because he is going to be sedentary for a while. The word "Down" should not be confused with "Get down" or "Off," which are the common misuses of the "Down" command. Think of "Get down" as a 1970s disco term and "Off" as a bug spray, not dog directions. If your dog jumps up on anything—the couch, you, or your guests—the correct word is simply "No."

The word "Down" in obedience training means lie down. If you want to teach your dog to lie down for an extended period of time you need to add the command "Stay" to your "Down" command, saying both words: "Stay Down." When the duration of time that you want your dog to remain down is over you need to release your dog with the word "O.K." Teaching your dog to lie down is equivalent to parking your car. It is important to implement the "Stay Down" command without distractions the first few times.

How to Teach Your Dog to Lie Down

1. Put the leash on your pooch.

2. Have your dog sit on your left-hand side.

3. Say "Stay."

4. Gather the leash in your right hand, so that there is a little tension.

5. Lift your left foot and *gently* step on the leash, saying the word "Down."

6. Keep your foot on the leash while repeating "Down." Your pup should lie down within a minute or two.

7. If he does not lie down right away, he is not afraid or being stubborn. He simply does not know what you want from him. Do not lift your foot unless your dog is really struggling. If he is, then lift your foot immediately, reach down to the buckle of the leash and pull on it three quick times, saying "No! No! No!" Begin again, from step one.

Your dog is looking to you for guidance. Repetition and consistency on your part will give both of you the confidence you need.

8. Do not lift your foot until he lies down. Keep your voice calm while saying the word "Down."

9.   Once your dog lies down, say "Good Down" in a mellow voice. Slowly lift your foot off the leash. You may get frustrated if he pops up. Hang in there and start again.

10.   If your dog remains down, slowly say "Stay Down." Lift your foot off the leash and step out in front of him. Praise him and wait a minute before returning to his side. He should be on your left side, still in the down position.

11.   Gently guide him up, lifting the leash, into a "Sit" position and say "Sit."

12.   Use your hand to draw your dog's eyes up to yours. Once you have eye contact, end the command by saying "O.K." in a happy voice.

COME: GIVING YOUR DOG THE GREEN LIGHT

The word "Come" should be a like a green flashing light, signaling your dog to run to you and sit eagerly in front of you until you release him with the "O.K." command. "Come" is the easiest command, although it can be the most difficult one to teach *people*, mainly because of the inconsistency with which they apply it.

The structure needed to formally teach your dog to come typically gets ruined the first day we bring our new pooch home. "Come here," is the first sentence out of our mouths, no matter what breed of dog owner we are. Yes, the ultimate desire of all dog owners is to have their dog come when they call.

However, "Come" can have a variety of meanings, because of how the command is used. For instance, "Come here" can mean come over here in this general area. Depending on your tone of voice, "Come here" can mean get over here right now, you are in big trouble. These different uses change "Come" to a yellow caution light instead of a green go signal for your dog. In fact, the effect can be that your dog will not come to you at all. The command "Come" must be formally taught on a leash in order to really isolate the word and connect it with an action.

How to Teach Your Dog the "Come" Command

1. Say "Sit" and then "Stay."

2. Using a long leash, walk six feet in front of your dog, turn around, and face him.

3. With a slight tug on the leash, take three steps backward, saying "Come" in an upbeat voice.

4. Stop and, as your dog comes toward you, guide him to "Sit."

5. Get eye contact with him, raising your hand to your eyes, then end the exercise with the release command "O.K.!"

For some people, learning to drive is easy. Others find it intimidating or complex. In working with your dog, your driving will depend largely on how well you apply the skills you learn. If you implement basic commands recklessly, without a leash, the result could be as devastating as running a red light and having an accident. Trying to train your dog to know the rules of the road while he is off leash will only give the dog whiplash, otherwise known as a mixed signal, or a mental jerk. On-leash commands must be conquered first before you can advance to off-leash. The following are ways that whiplash can occur.

Whiplash: Giving Mixed Signals

1. Do not attempt to train your dog off leash before your dog knows the commands on leash. Off-leash, he doesn't have to listen to you because there are no restraints . Off-leash, you're out of luck if he gets distracted or doesn't want to obey. Plus, the action of disobeying is allowed to occur, creating a pattern of its own.

2. Do not push down your dog's butt while commanding him to "Sit." Push down on your dog and he'll automatically resist. Your dog's focus switches from the command to your hand on his rear.

3. Do not speed through the training process by misusing treats. The dog is eager to get the treat. The emphasis shifts from the command itself to solely the reward.

4. Do not use a command as a reprimand. Your dog won't perceive a direction as a way of pleasing you, only as a form of discipline.

Teaching your dog the basic commands of "Heel," "Sit," "Stay," "Down," and "Come" allows you both to cruise along and enjoy the scenery. Now that you have had your driving lesson, get ready to go for your license. Keep reading and find out where to incorporate all of the basics into your everyday life.

Heel Thyself

To err is human, to forgive, canine.
—ANONYMOUS

Yes, heel thyself is a pun, a simple reminder that good training takes two—your dog and you—with the emphasis on *you* to make it fun. In the last chapter, I discussed how to apply basic obedience commands. Many dog owners assume that once their dog starts to perform a specific task, school is out. Wrong. It is crucial to do the homework.

You must practice all of the basic commands in the locations where you most want your dog to behave, with all the distractions of those places. Real-life distractions include doorbells, guests, delivery people, food, children, other dogs, and even cats. Teaching your dog to pay attention to you amid life's distractions is always challenging and often frustrating. However, it can be made simple if you use a leash for consistency, practice just a few minutes a day, and apply the techniques from Chapter 8. Where and when you apply the training in your home is the key to creating a positive behavior pattern.

Don't wait until your dog jumps up on guests or bolts out the front door after the pizza delivery guy. Instead, try rehearsing "Sit" and "Stay" at an open front door with no one around. Practice ringing the doorbell, too.

Behaviors take time to develop. This chapter will address how to use training to your advantage and prevent some doggy delinquencies from developing in the first place.

VOICE INFLECTION

Some of the sweetest people can end up cursing like sailors, quickly turning the obedience command into a reprimand rather than positive communication. Other dog owners say nothing, but give their dogs the silent disapproval of the Ol' Evil Eye glare. The key to positive reinforcement is having a pleasant voice when giving obedience commands.

Some people constantly coo at their dogs, except when they implement a command like "Stay" or "Heel." Then the firm I-mean-business voice comes out, signaling punishment rather than praise to the dog.

In your role as puppy parent, think about playing Mary Poppins with an edge. I coined this phrase to help explain the attitude and voice inflection needed to implement a command. Use the kind, pleasant voice of Mary Poppins and add an "edge" of guidance, given with quick snaps of the leash when heeling. The tone of your voice when you give a dog a command tells him whether he is pleasing you or not, and he aims to please. So make learning a happy experience.

In your role as a puppy parent, you've got to think about playing Mary Poppins with an edge.

Simple Solutions
It is important not to speak to your dog in a stern or monotone voice. Put emphasis on the command itself, not your dog's name. Always praise your dog during a command and afterward as well.

The Whiner Breed of Dog Owner's Complaint
Q. My dog knows not to get on the couch. I constantly tell him to get off, but he gives me a blank look and ignores me. Is he doing this to spite me?

A. No, dogs do not lie on couches to spite their owners. They lie on couches because they can. If you are not clear in your voice inflection and are inconsistent in your actions, he really does not understand what you want. You are probably whining at your dog in ways that would confuse any Cocker Spaniel. You cannot assume your dog knows what you mean. Your voice inflection needs to clearly express your displeasure. If you don't want your dog on the couch, he needs to hear a quick, firm "No!" Then provide an alternative place, such as a dog bed or a big towel to curl up on. Guide him to the spot with a bone for him to chew. This shows him where he is supposed to be while you're watching TV. This sets a positive precedent.

HEEL: WALKING THE DOG

It is a great habit to go on daily walks with your dog. It is good exercise for both of you. We all have a tendency to wrap the leash tightly in our hand and hang on for dear life. This habit causes your dog to pull even more. The tighter you hold the leash, the more your dog is going to pull.

Simple Solutions
The first place to teach your dog to "Heel," believe it or not, is in your living room. There are fewer distractions in your house than on the street, enabling you both to focus. Heeling in your living room, as crazy as it seems, allows your pooch to accomplish the command successfully, with eye contact. Remember to use the leash and training collar.

The second place to practice "Heel" is walking out the front door, as if you're going for a walk. Then you turn and walk back in. In other words, heel up and down your front walk, breaking your dog's old behavior of always dragging you out the door and down the street. Your pup may look at you as though you are from the planet Pluto, but this exercise will break the pattern.

Another way to stop the pattern of pulling is to guide your dog to "Sit" more often. For example, take a few steps at a time saying "Heel," then stop and say "Sit." Doing this repeatedly will cause your dog to pay attention to your unpredictable pace, and to learn to watch for your next step. Don't forget to give lots of quick snaps of the leash and keep using an encouraging voice while saying the word "Heel." If your dog is really energetic, exercise that high-powered pup first, by playing fetch. A pooped pup will make the heeling process more successful while you are both still learning.

Remember, walking your dog is much like driving a car. If your dog has the energy of a Ferrari, then drive with authority.

The O.K. Breed of Dog Owner's Complaint

Q. I have a Labrador retriever that thinks every walk is the Iditarod sled race. I'm embarrassed! I have to pretend that I'm a dog musher from Alaska every time I take my dog for a walk. Any suggestions, aside from getting Rollerblades?

A. Well, sled dog owner, this is not O.K., even with skates. You need to think "follow the leader." Except *you* need to be the leader, not your pooch. When he starts to pull you down the street, switch directions and say "Let's go" or "Heel" in a pleasant voice. It's that easy. A quick pivot in the opposite direction, along with a quick snap of the leash and some praise will do the trick. Indicate with occasional snaps of the leash the speed at which you want to walk, and keep up the praise. Dogs are pack animals, they will follow your lead. Besides, your dog doesn't have a choice—he's on a leash.

Heeling in your living room creates the pattern of how you want your dog to behave. It also allows you to accomplish the command successfully with eye contact.

STAY

The command "Stay" is needed most at the front door, when guests arrive. Some people go to extreme lengths and have to play a game of touch football with their dog to prevent him from bolting outside. You can actually break a sweat during this form of training.

A common fascination of owners is to see if their dog will actually obey a "Stay" command off leash in this situation. It won't work, until you have drilled the dog so often that the distraction of the doorbell and guests becomes insignificant to him. Remember, "Stay" means "Do not move until I release you with the word O.K." Do not use the word "Stay" when leaving the house. It should only be used when you want the dog to remain without moving for a brief period of time, in your presence.

Simple Solutions

I recommend that you practice the "Stay" command in your house without any distractions for a few minutes twice a day. Over a period of a week, gradually increase the amount of time and the number of distractions. (See Chapter 8 steps for the "Stay" command.)

The Control Freak's Complaint

Q. My dog has his own way of greeting guests at the front door. When the doorbell rings, he turns from Lassie into Cujo. I welcome my friends by yelling "No! Get down!" at my dog and then apologizing to my friends. It's chaos.

A. This situation may seem beyond control, but Cujo can change. Don't try to discipline your dog with angry commands during a cocktail party. Dogs learn much faster through positive reinforcement, so try this when you are both undistracted. Put your pooch on a leash and implement the "Stay" command while having a café au lait moment. On a Sunday morning while relaxing, implement the command for a few minutes with no distractions. It will work, if you are both calm and mellow, with no distractions, and able to accomplish the command from beginning to end successfully. Then gradually add distractions.

Ask a friend or family member to visit on a Saturday afternoon with a treat in hand. Keep a leash by the door. When the doorbell rings, put your dog on the leash and guide him to "Sit" and "Stay." Open the door and have your friend also guide him to "Stay" and then give him the treat while he continues to stay. (Be careful the treat is not held so high that your dog has to jump up to get it.) Then release him with "O.K." This exercise will train your dog in a positive way to greet your friends with civility.

PAW PRINT: Man's habit of feeding dogs table scraps has been around since the time when wolves would scavenge prehistoric man's kills.

DOWN

"Down" is the most misused command. People say "Get down" to order their dog off the bed. They say "No, down!" and mean "Please do not jump on me." Or they say "Go lie down," which doesn't mean rest but, actually, "Buzz off." If you have used the command in these ways, just think how confused your dog must be.

The command "Down" should mean only one thing to you and your dog, and that is to lie down. Initially, practice the command with your dog on a leash in your house, at a time when there are few distractions. Eventually you can use this command at an outside café.

Simple Solutions

Implement the command formally, going through the twelve steps, as explained in Chapter 8. While your dog is staying down, sit in a nearby chair. This will be quite a distraction for him. Seeing you at rest will entice your dog to try to play with you and break the "Stay." Start with short periods of time, one or two minutes, increasing to five minutes, then to twenty minutes or more the following week. This is all part of working the dog into your lifestyle.

Next, apply the "Down" command while you are sitting and eating a sandwich. Be sure to say "Stay Down" if you want him to remain lying down for a while. Initially, use the "Stay Down" command when you're having a snack rather than a long, fancy feast.

Places at Home to Practice "Stay Down" on a Leash
- In the kitchen while you prepare food
- At the dining table while you eat
- In the living room while you are watching TV

Your dog's age and maturity will determine the length of time it will take to master the "Stay Down" command. Do not expect a four-month-old pup to hold a "Stay Down" through a two-hour movie on TV. Once again, it is wise to tire an active dog by playing fetch with him before practicing this command. Do not try to teach your pooch the "Down" command when he is rambunctious.

If you try to implement the command on a puppy that is not mature enough to hold a stay for twenty minutes, he will constantly break it. If you become aggravated, this creates a negative experience for your dog.

On those occasions when you do not want to use a leash and practice a formal command like "Stay Down," an option is to crate your dog with a chew bone while you are relaxing in the same room. This is not a punishment. It simply will set a precedent for your dog to relax while you relax. This is just an option, not a replacement for the "Stay Down" command. Always remember to exercise your pup before you crate him, and to guide him in and out of the crate on a leash. Crate for short periods of time only. Later the "Down" command can be accompanied by a dog bed next to your favorite chair and you can both watch reruns of *Lassie*.

 PAW PRINT: The hound group contains some of the oldest breeds known to man. The Greyhound, being the fastest, reaches speeds of up to 37 mph.

COME

Most of us try to teach our new puppy to come by crouching and saying "Come here" while clapping our hands. It may appear as though your pup is responding to the word "Come" when, in fact, he is tracking your body language and voice inflection, not the word "Come" itself. You believe that your dog comprehends the command off-leash, when he does not. You could be saying the word

"Margarita" (while dreaming about one to calm your own nerves), but it really wouldn't matter.

Your pup is merely responding to your voice inflection, rather than to the word "Come."

Trying to teach your dog to come off leash can be exasperating because it doesn't always work. Just when you are convinced your dog will come when called, off he runs. By the time the pup reaches adolescence, it seems he has no clue what the word may mean. Constantly repeating a command that your dog is not responding to only encourages him to continue his bad behavior.

Simple Solutions

There are many different ways to get your dog to come to you, but only one way to formally teach your dog the command "Come." Learning which method is right for each circumstance becomes the challenge.

Practice "Stay" and "Come" formally on a leash outside the front door, asking your dog to come to you as you take several steps backward, leading your dog into the house through the front door. Then say "Sit," formally end the command with the word "O.K.," and give him lots of love. Ending all commands is important because it indicates to your pup a job well done.

Practicing "Come" at your front doorway, on a leash, creates a positive pattern. It shows your dog exactly what you want most, which is for him to come into the house when called. Another area to practice the "Come" command is at the gate leading out of your yard, also a common trouble spot.

The Talker's Complaint

Q. I tell my dog to come in the house because it's getting late, but he just ignores me. I explain that I am going to a movie and I will be back in a couple of hours. He still doesn't budge. I always have to go and get him, or entice him with a biscuit to get him in from the backyard. Why doesn't my dog understand "Come"?

A. Do you think the words, "Come here right now I need you in the house because I am going to a movie and I am going to be late" are the same as the "Come" command? Think again. Reciting the encyclopedia is not going to get your dog to come to you any faster or be any smarter. You need to know when to practice the formal "Come" command. Or where to apply other, less formal techniques.

All of the methods below are options that will work in different everyday circumstances. Too many bad human habits will delay the progress of your dog's natural response to these exercises, so watch yourself. If your dog does not respond, then you need to undo some of the bad habits that have been created. Go back to the basics and reread Chapter 8.

Three informal techniques to get your dog to "Come"

1. *Using Body Language.* Crouch down and clap your hands, using enthusiasm and friendly body language. Then, with a happy voice, praise your dog *without* saying the word "Come." Your pup will gladly trot over to you, prompted by your voice inflection and inviting posture. This is most effective with really young puppies.

This tip teaches dog owners to be smarter than their young pups. It gets the desired result of your dog coming to you, without enforcing a command that has not yet been introduced into the pup's vocabulary.

2. *Reverse Psychology: Running in the Opposite Direction.* A bad habit is to walk toward our dog while angrily saying the word "Come," causing the dog to run the other way. Does that make sense?

Many owners have a difficult time getting their pet to come to them when the dog is enjoying himself in a dog park. In a park with dogs, children, and other distractions, it's helpful to use reverse psychology, rather than trying to enforce a formal command. Get your dog's attention by calling his name and then bolt in the opposite direction. The movement will spur your dog to chase you. While running, turn around to face your dog. Stop and guide him into a "Sit." As your dog sits, hold his attention by guiding his eyes up to yours, then release him with the command "O.K." Give him lots of love.

Dogs have a natural inclination to chase and catch, called a prey drive. This exercise teaches you how to productively use the dog's innate drive for your own benefit.

3.   *Hide-and-Seek*. Hide-and-seek is a fun name-recognition game. The game teaches your dog to seek you out when you use his name. Too many dog owners constantly repeat their dog's name without specifying what they really want from the dog. Before long, the dog tunes them out. Seeking you out of hiding gives your dog a fun action to perform while hearing his name called. It also cures dog owners of their bad habit of using the dog's name aimlessly.

It is very important that you initiate this game in your house, not outside. The game needs to be played indoors for safety reasons. The boundaries of your home allow you and your dog to experience success with this game without distractions, creating a pattern of success and fun.

How to Play the Game of Hide-and-Seek

•   One person holds the dog by its collar. The other person gets a treat and hides.

•   The person hiding calls the dog's name enthusiastically and repeatedly, clapping his or her hands and making a big deal out of the dog's name.

•   The person holding the dog should remain silent and let go of the dog the third time the dog is called.

•   The person hiding should continue calling the dog's name until found.

•   When your dog finds you, stand up. Guide your dog into a "Sit," using the treat. As your dog sits waiting for the treat, draw the treat up close to your eyes. Get eye contact with the dog. Then say "O.K." and give the pup his treat.

Hide-and-seek teaches your dog to seek you out, prompted by hearing his name called. This reinforces name recognition and teaches your dog to come to you when he hears his name. The key to hide-and-seek is that you must be out of sight when calling your dog. Hide-and-seek must have a beginning, middle, and end.

PAW PRINT: The canine Frisbee championship created in 1975 in the United States was a legacy to a dog named Ashley Whippet, a canine with a great leaping ability.

TAIL WAG: KEVIN COSTNER

Getting your young pup to come to you off leash from a distance while distracted can be difficult. You're not alone. Actor-director Kevin Costner and his family had a similar problem with their beautiful Labrador, Wyatt. This precocious pup gave the phrase "dances with wolves" a new meaning. Wyatt was untouchable when he was called, especially while being distracted by the Costner kids swimming in their pool. He would zip past you as if he were chasing an Oscar for *Bone* Durham. One way of solving this problem was to teach everyone in the family the game of hide-and-seek. It was a great way for Costner's children to direct Wyatt to come when called and to still have fun. Wyatt learned to turn on a dime when hearing his name, come to you, sit, and wait for his next cue. Proof that in Hollywood, there *can* be more than one top dog in a family. For Wyatt, obedience was a wrap.

DISTRACTIONS

Life is a distraction. The objective of basic obedience commands—Heel, Sit, Stay, Come, and Down—is to be able to apply them within the context of daily life distractions, not in an obedience ring. What are distractions? Well, they vary. To a three-month-old puppy, a leaf blowing across the sidewalk is a distraction. To an adolescent dog, who has been-there-done-that, a leaf in the wind is old news—but a boy on a bike must be chased!

It's safe to say that movement of any kind is a distraction. A cat running across the street or guests at the front door increases the degree of difficulty when you are trying to apply an obedience command. Smells are also a major distraction, whether the scent of another dog on your guest's trousers or your sandwich on the coffee table.

This may sound obvious, but listen again: It is imperative that you take into account the many distractions around you while applying basic obedience training. That's where the magic of a well-behaved dog lies. It's crucial that you teach your dog on a leash. Conditioning is important in order to keep your dog's focus when a real guest is at the front door. Believe me, your dog will have the same reaction to the sound of the doorbell whether someone is there or not.

You can also practice the "Stay" command on a leash and throw a ball as a distraction. The ball will have the same effect as the movement of a cat running across the street. Simulating different sounds, smells, and movements in a controlled environment will help you advance your dog to "hold" commands while he becomes accustomed to our busy, hectic, and unpredictable daily life.

I hope this chapter has given a new awareness to the "good" human habits we can create by applying basic obedience to our daily routine, which will lead our dogs to be well-mannered. Now, let's find out how we can solve some unusual canine quirks.

Fifteen Things You Didn't Want to Know about Your Dog . . . but Now You Do

Life is just a bowl of cherries.
—TITLE OF SONG BY LOU BROWN AND
RAY HENDERSON

Now that you have read all about your dog-owner quirks and habits, you'll find that you are not alone. Most likely you have discovered that your dog has acquired a few quirks of his own. The following are fifteen things that you probably never cared to know about dogs before you were a dog owner, but now, as a dog parent, you do.

1. Why Do Some Dogs Eat Cat Poop?
Answer: Why do some people eat snails?

Dogs may consider cat poop a delicacy. Its high ash content makes it a tempting treat for some dogs.

Advice: Try one or more of the following:

• Move the kitty litter to an area that you can baby-gate so your cat can jump over the gate but your dog cannot get in.

• Get a kitty litter box that has a hood on it, and place the opening of the litter toward the wall, so just your cat can get in but your dog cannot.

2. Yuck! Even Worse! Why Does My Puppy Eat His Own Poop?

Answer: It could be because of a dietary deficiency. This habit is more common than you think. Luckily, most puppies grow out of it.

Advice: Keep his bathroom area clean. Check with your vet about his diet or any health disorders, like worms. Ask your vet for FORBID, a food supplement that you add to your puppy's food that makes poop taste bad. Feel free to say "No!" to him when you see him eating what he shouldn't.

3. Why Does My Dog Bark His Head Off in the Backyard Every Evening Between 5:30 and 7:00?

Answer: Because he can and he's a dog. He hears people in the neighborhood coming home from work, as well as others walking their dogs.

Advice: Take him inside for a rest or for a walk and he won't bark.

4. Why Does My Dog Refuse to Eat His Food? I Have Tried 101 Different Kinds of Kibble and Canned Foods and Nothing Works.

Answer: Too many choices. Your dog is not a cat. Also, do not leave his food out all day.

Advice: Dogs do not become anorexic. Check with your vet to make sure your dog is healthy. If you're feeding him any human food at all, *you* have created his finicky eating pattern. Time-feed your dog. He may remain finicky and not eat for a day or so, but a healthy dog will eat on the second day. Leave the food in his bowl for twenty minutes. Hang out with your dog while he eats. If he doesn't finish his food, remove the bowl until the next feeding. This will create a pattern of eating at a designated mealtime.

5. Why Does My Dog Sniff Every Blade of Grass on Our Walk? It Drives Me Nuts. What is He Looking For?

Answer: Quite honestly, it is his way of reading a magazine before he poops. A dog's nose tells a tale of what's been on that path. A dog's sense of smell is approximately 100,000 times greater than ours.

Advice: Let him smell until he relieves himself. Then be smarter than your dog and guide him to walk at your side.

6. Why Does My Four-Month-Old Puppy Bite Me Constantly? I Say "No," Yet He Just Will Not Leave Me Alone.

Answer: All of his baby teeth are falling out and adult teeth are growing in. Chewing is a function of a dog. What he chews on becomes a behavior over time.

Advice: Do not wave your hands in front of him, as this only entices him to bite them. Some people can be their own worst enemies. They insist on giving their puppy affection, while at the same time saying "No!" for biting them. Tire your puppy with exercise first, give him a bone to chew, and then cuddle with him.

7. My Puppy Knows Exactly Where the Dog Door Is. Why Doesn't She Use it?

Answer: Your puppy has to be taught to use it by you.

Advice: Put your pup on a leash. Have a treat in your hand. Throw the treat through the dog door, then gently lift your pup through the dog door opening. As she is lifted through the dog door, she will find the treat on the other side. Then gently pull the leash, calling her name in a happy voice, and pull her back inside. Give her another treat and say "Good dog!" Have patience.

8. Why Does My Three-Month-Old Puppy Scratch His Neck All the Time? I Know He Does Not Have Fleas.

Answer: Is he wearing a new collar? If so, that's why. It is similar to having a ring on your finger for the first time. It feels funny and may itch, at first.

Advice: If your puppy is not wearing a collar and is still itching, check with your vet.

9. Why Do Dogs Bite Each Other When They Play?

Answer: Why did humans invent the game of football? Although it may look rough at times, when dogs bite, nip, and wrestle with one another, it is their way of having a fun time.

Advice: As the owner of one of the players, you should make sure it's a fair game. Keep an eye out to make sure it doesn't get too aggressive.

10. Why Do I Need to Spay or Neuter My Dog? I Have Heard That it Is Better for My Dog to Have One Litter.

Answer: The number of homeless dogs is astronomical. Do your part to help control this problem by having your own pet spayed or neutered. I had no problem with getting my female dog spayed. However, some people project their own issues onto their dogs, and feel that they would not want to be spayed or neutered themselves.

Advice: Get over it. Having puppies is a lot of work. If you don't believe me, go read a book on how to breed your dog: it isn't pretty. I also suggest going to your local shelter to see some of the thousands of homeless dogs waiting to be killed, due to humans' failure to spay and neuter. The figures are staggering. Some eleven to seventeen million pets are euthanized in the United States each year. This is partly due to backyard breeding, but it is mainly the result of owner irresponsibility and a lack of education. If you're still not convinced about neutering, ask your vet about the many health risks, such as testicular cancers and a host of behavioral issues, including potential dog aggression, which can develop in unneutered dogs.

Many people have asked me if spaying or neutering will make their dog fat and lazy or change his or her personality. I would like you to look my lean, one-hundred-pound German shepherd (who was neutered at the age of six months) in the eye and tell him that he is fat or lazy. The only things that will make your dog fat are overfeeding and lack of exercise. *Please* take responsibility and get your dog fixed. Do research and educate yourself. Leave breeding to professionals.

11. How Do I Stop My Dog from Jumping up on My Guests?

Answer: Some dogs jump up, some goose, and others slobber on your friends to say hello.

Unless the dog is middle-aged or geriatric, that's just what dogs do. You can yell "No!" or apologize profusely, but what you need to do is condition your pooch. Dogs learn quickly through positive reinforcement.

Advice: Don't try to correct this behavior during a party. If it has become a pet peeve then use a little foresight and gate your dog prior to your guests' arrival. Make sure the dog's needs are met and gate him with a new bone.

12. My Dog Barks Like a Machine Gun Going off When the Doorbell Rings. Now I Have a New Baby, and This Is a Real Problem. What Can I do?

Answer: This behavior usually sneaks up on dog owners. It develops as your dog matures. Some dogs are louder and more alert than others. To a first-time dog owner, when a dog is eight months old or so, the first barks at the doorbell are kind of cute. Later, it's annoying.

Advice: Remember that dogs don't bark when the phone rings because there is no special stimulation attached. When the doorbell rings there is always someone for your dog to greet, and this stimulates the barking. Condition your dog to ignore the doorbell just as he refuses to answer the phone. Put your dog on a leash and open the door and ring the doorbell repeatedly until he pays attention to you when you guide him to "Sit" at the door. A second option is to make a penny can, gate your dog and then go and ring the doorbell. As your dog begins to bark, shake the penny can once and say "No!" Repeat this exercise until the barking at the doorbell stops. Then return to him and praise him for sitting. Voilà! In time your dog will turn back into Lassie.

 PAW PRINT: George Washington owned 37 dogs.

13. How Do I Get My Dog Not to Snoop in the Trash? My Dog Only Goes in the Trash When I'm Not in the Room or I'm Away from Home. Why Is This?

Answer: Your dog is being a dog. He does this when you are not home because your presence represents authority. And when the cat's away, the dog will play.

Advice: You can use a combination of the following methods. Be smarter than your dog. Put the trash away, or put a heavy lid on the trash can and call it a day. Don't yell "No!" at your dog randomly. It never solves this problem. You can formally reprimand your dog by putting him on a leash and guiding him silently over to the trash. Put his nose near the trash, not in it, and say "No." Then guide your dog over to a chew bone and say "O.K." Then take off the leash and the reprimand is over.

14. What Can I Do to Stop Excessive Barking from the Backyard?

Answer: This is probably the most common behavior problem and, to some degree, it is quite normal. Not all dogs who bark at other dogs from the backyard become aggressive. But, depending on temperament, training, and the number of the dogs you own, it can lead to dog aggression. This innocent barking stems from dogs' territorialism—protecting their turf—which is innate.

Advice: Most people feel that when their dog barks it is doing its job. If you leave your dog in the backyard all day, then this barking can be due to boredom. It is common and is called—you guessed it—boredom barking. This type of behavior is often ignored and how well you deal with it usually depends on your mood. Don't give your dog mixed signals combined with inconsistent corrections. Make a decision about actually correcting your dog rather than yelling the random "No!" at him.

Here are some useful suggestions:

• Do not leave your dog in the backyard for lengthy periods. Bring him indoors and break the pattern.

• Cover the fence with canvas so your dog cannot see out, or build a wooden fence.

• Use your instincts about your dog's temperament and listen to the tone of the bark. Is he protecting the yard against another dog? Or is the barking from the anxiety of wanting to come inside? Respond accordingly.

• Tire him out and bring him inside. A tired dog is a calm dog.

• If you have a little dog and the bark is a warning alert of another dog approaching, then a simple shake of a penny can while you are out of sight will do the trick.

• If you have a dog that sounds like he is going to kill the dog on the other side of the fence, it could be the beginning of a serious behavioral problem, such as dog aggression. Read Chapter 11, "Working Out the Kinks."

15. My New Puppy Is Tormenting My Cat. How Can I Help Them Get Along?

<u>**Answer:**</u> This takes time. Your puppy and cat need to acclimate to each other's smells and movements. When your pup goes through his teething stage, it is best to gate him with a chew bone. This allows your cat time to walk around, and your puppy to get used to your cat's presence.

<u>**Advice:**</u> The baby gate is your best tool for helping both pets to get used to each other. This does not mean keeping your dog gated at all times. It means you can sometimes gate your cat, giving your puppy free time, and vice versa. In time the two will learn to live together and you can keep your sanity.

Also, remember that your cat can choose to jump over the gate and socialize, or keep its privacy behind the gate.

CHAPTER

11

Working Out the Kinks

Don't give up. Don't lose hope. Don't sell out.
—CHRISTOPHER REEVE

O.K., you're slowly realizing that the honeymoon stage of your relationship with your dog is screeching to a halt. Maybe your dog isn't Bill Gates or Einstein after all. You're running into some kinks. These kinks are most likely just growing pains, meaning that your dog has hit a new stage of development.

By the time the dog is eight months old, your wonder child has become the wild child. You can't believe his stupidity. Chasing cats across the street has become his favorite pastime—while you, now a more seasoned dog parent, may consider popping Prozac.

Actually, your dog is just being a dog. Many owners did not guide their new dog from day one through the basics, and now certain behaviors have become the last straw. Others start at this stage, working out the kinks, because they have adopted a pound pup that is already a teenager, and they wing it until a bad behavior develops. If this is the case, and you have flipped directly to this chapter due to your dog's misdeeds, be sure to go back and read what you have missed. As in any relationship, sometimes you have to take three steps backward before you can move one step ahead.

Depending on your pet's disposition, some of you have just driven in reverse the whole time, and have a few bones to pick with your dog. After about six months together, the road can get rocky. Some of you might be thinking, "Why me? All I wanted was the hangin' hound. I have spent a zillion dollars on beds, bones, crates, and gates, and my dog is still stealing my sandwich." Whether your dog is excessively barking, digging, or begging, this chapter deals with working out the kinks.

By now you have probably figured out that you are the one who's being trained. Whether you have one bone to pick with your dog or a smorgasbord of issues, you should know one thing: You CAN teach an old dog new tricks.

This brings to mind a story about a nine-year-old pug named Junior. His owner, a busy television executive named Reed, had been cleaning up, or stepping in, the "occasional accident" for NINE years. Good thing Junior wasn't a Great Dane! The reasons given for this problem were bountiful. Reed worked long hours, felt guilty, and believed Junior was getting even with him for spending time with his girlfriend. It wasn't until Reed bought a house and his girlfriend (with two cats) became his fiancée that I got the call, an emergency 911 PUG call.

"You are my last hope," said Reed. "We have to get Junior to stop peeing in our new house. I know Junior can hold it all day because sometimes he does, and other times he doesn't." Feeling a little like Clark Kent, I went to their new house and explained the principles of applying positive boundaries. I taught both Reed and his fiancée the information found in Chapters 5 and 6, sprinkled with a short sermon on the philosophy of patience. Two short months later, Reed called, sounding happy and relieved. "Junior defies all myths that you can't train an old dog to do new tricks," he said. "Junior is so much happier now that he is pleasing both of his masters. Thank you." This was music to my ears, for Junior's sake as well as Reed's.

In this chapter I will offer solutions to seven of the most common behavioral problems for dog owners. All the information in this chapter is built on the foundation of basic obedience. Therefore, I hope you and your pup have a good handle on the basic commands of "Heel," "Sit," "Stay," "Come," and "Down" before you start working out the kinks. Remember, the rewards can be wonderful, so put the energy into sticking it out for the long haul.

CAUTION
All of the behavior modification described in this chapter must be adapted to individual circumstances and a dog's temperament and background. In extreme cases, you should call a professional trainer or behaviorist to specifically address individual issues with your dog.

Bone to Pick: My First Dog Is Lassie; My Second Dog Is a Pain in the—!

Adding a second dog can mean double trouble, depending on your lifestyle. It is a common but odd thing that happens. The minute you get your first dog trained, the compulsion is to rock the boat again and get another one. I did it, and so have many of my clients. My recommendation is not to get a second dog simply for the sake of keeping your first dog company. Only get one if you want to raise another dog.

Initially, it is double the work. I think the best combination is a male and a female, even though I have seen successful combinations of both two females and two males. It is helpful for your first dog to be older than the second one, since you already will have an understanding with the first one, and can focus on raising the second dog. Getting littermates can be double trouble.

A natural pecking order should emerge, with you as the leader. A younger second dog should naturally submit to your first dog. Your first dog should remain dominant, although not aggressive, over the new pup.

After getting married to her famous actor-director husband, Jason, Ashlee Petersen Priestley didn't waste any time adding a new member to the family. The busy household already included her five-year-old son, a goldfish, and a five-year old French Bulldog called Swifty. Then Ashlee added Hudson, a Rhodesian Ridgeback to the menagerie. She hoped that Hudson would just follow Swifty's lead out the dog door and housebreak himself with minimum effort. After a month of waiting for Hudson to get it, things got worse.

The new dog began having more "mistakes" in the house, including chewing the furniture. The two dogs started arguing over bones, with Swifty the usual winner, leaving Hudson with nothing to chew (except the couch, of course)! Even when the floor was covered with bones, each dog wanted only the bone that the other one had. Ashlee, a lifelong dog owner, called me for help.

Hudson was already a four-month-old, forty-five-pound good pup with bad habits. I explained the gating theory (see Chapters 5 and 6) to Ashlee and helped her organize a daily routine, with a potty schedule, and set up a gating system that gave each dog its special bone time. This reduced competition between the two dogs and helped Ashlee manage the process of housebreaking Hudson exclusively. The first few days were challenging, but Ashlee followed the rules. The outcome of this doubles game was set, love, and match.

People Training

In whatever ball game you've got going, here are some broad guidelines to use when you throw a curve ball to your first dog by adding a second. On the first day, when you bring the new pup home, follow the baby-gating technique (see Chapter 5, "Creating Positive Boundaries"). This will avert all sorts of potential problems and show both of your dogs that you are in charge.

It is not fair to either dog to let your new puppy invade your older dog's space immediately. If your first dog is not happy initially, the baby gate will allow everyone to adjust to the idea of having a new family member. Relationships take time to develop. The gate also affords your new pup chewing time without competition. Your first dog should be able to have some relief from a teething puppy. If your new puppy is teething, it must have plenty of chew toys without having to forfeit them to your older dog, and you should not have to referee.

If your puppy growls at your older dog, which is rare (but I have seen it happen), you need to stop the behavior. Sometimes a very dominant young puppy will try to flex his muscles, so to speak, over a feeble older dog. Definitely separate them. The age difference may be too extreme for them to be playmates. If so, it is up to you to meet your new pup's needs so that he does not make a hobby out of pestering your older dog.

You need to alternate gating time for the two of them. Give your puppy free time while your older dog is gated, and vice versa. This might be confusing at first for your older dog, but it will enable them to get used to each other safely. Training the new pup is essential, although his attention may wander, due to the constant distraction of your first dog. Gating will help you organize quality time with each dog until harmony develops.

Give them supervised play time at first, so that you can correct any behavioral issues that may develop. During their free time together, it is helpful not to leave any toys or bones lying around; that way they can't fight over them. Feed them separately, perhaps with a baby gate between them, for several months. This will eliminate competition and possessiveness.

Double Trouble

• Do not get a dog for the sole purpose of keeping your first dog company. The only good reason for adding another dog is that you want another dog and you are willing to do the work of caring for two dogs.

• Do not allow a new puppy to dominate or bully an older dog. It is up to you to set the rules. Use your judgment regarding your older dog's limitations with a new, teething pup. Separate them with a baby gate when your puppy gets too rambunctious.

• For several weeks, or months, depending on the age of your new dog, do not leave the dogs together unsupervised. Gate the new dog and train him as you did the first one.

• If your older dog growls, reprimand this behavior with a firm "No!" or, in extreme cases, give a shake of the penny can.

Bone to Pick: My Dog Steals Food When My Back Is Turned, What Should I do?
You're starving. You sit down to eat a great sandwich and there are those sad eyes staring at you. The drool starts dripping out of

the corner of your dog's mouth. Your chewing slows down and you begin to feel guilty for eating your own sandwich. You get up for some ketchup and when you come back the dog has snatched your sandwich and is finishing the last bite.

This happened to the Norton family. Their dainty diva Daisy, a Standard Poodle, began to develop a not-so-refined habit of snatching an occasional snack off the kitchen counter. The day of a family barbecue, Daisy's habit became dangerous. While snooping around the picnic table, she picked up the wrong snack, a barbecued chicken leg. (Chicken bones can be very harmful to dogs.) Fortunately, the Nortons outsmarted Daisy and got the chicken bone before she swallowed it. Here are the same suggestions I gave them on how to teach Daisy not to have such delinquent delicacies.

You can yell "No!" at your dog until the cows come home, but a dog will still be a dog. This is where dog owners really begin to feel righteous. Their dog knows not to steal food. They believe this mainly because the dog does not always do it in front of them.

People Training

Have you given your dog any human food? If you have, you cannot have it both ways. Buy your dog as many expensive dog treats as you want, but if you occasionally share food with him, or flip him potato chips, do not complain when he becomes a food thief. *No human food!* Here are four training tips on how to curb this behavior once it has developed. Consistency and follow-through are very important. Each training suggestion caters to a specific dog-owner mood and is designed to be easily incorporated into your daily routine.

Four Ways to Stop Your Dog from Stealing Food

1.   *Use Foresight:* Many times we are not in the mood to practice formal training with our dog during a meal. Therefore we do nothing and allow our dog's begging, drooling, or stealing of food to continue. If you're not in the mood to do a formal command, use foresight and gate your dog before you eat. Apply the command "Wait" when gating your dog. (See Chapter 5.)

(a) Guide your dog into the gated area on a leash to formalize the routine. This also keeps you from having to force or coax your dog into an area.

(b) Say, "Sit, Wait," then put up the baby gate. Take off the leash and give him a chew bone or pig's ear.

2. *Apply the "Stay" command:* If you have the time on a weekend afternoon, apply the command "Stay" while eating a sandwich. Putting your dog in a "Stay" will help him get used to being around human food and behaving himself at the same time.
Give your dog some exercise—make sure he is a little tired.

(a) Put your dog on a leash.

(b) Guide him into a sit by lifting up on the leash.

(c) Say "Stay" and then sit down yourself approximately one leash length away from your dog and eat a sandwich.

(d) Get ready for some exercise because your dog will break the "Stay" command a lot. Simply sitting in a chair can make you quite a distraction for your dog, who'll think it's time to play. Eating a sandwich makes you all the more a distraction. Your incorporating this obedience exercise into your daily routine will make all the difference in your dog's behavior around food.
Your body language is more dominant when you are standing in front of your dog staring at him, repeating a command, then when you are sitting in a chair preoccupied with eating a snack. Do not expect your new dog to behave like Lassie immediately. Incorporating the advanced "Stay" command with distractions, takes time. It is a process.

(e) If your dog breaks the "Stay" command, get up saying nothing. Reach for the clasp of the leash and jerk the leash three times, saying "No! No! No!" and then, in a pleasant voice, repeat "Sit. Stay." Sit down in the chair again and resume eating. If he gets up again, repeat the whole process. You have to be in the mood to do this!

3.   *Cooking with your pooch?* While you're cooking in the kitchen, put your dog on a leash and tie the leash to your belt. Every time you stop to do something, just say "Sit." This will help him to get accustomed to food smells, as well as to minding his manners at the same time. This sets a precedent for how you want him to behave. If he jumps on the counter, since he is on a leash you can snap the leash and say "No!" in a firm voice. Then follow with "Sit." You can even bang your hand on the counter, making a loud noise, to really bring the point home.

4.   *The setup:* Put a handful of pennies in an empty coffee can and close the plastic lid. Have it ready in the kitchen. Put your dog on a leash, then bait your dog by putting a piece of cheese on a plate on the kitchen table. Hang out in the kitchen doing something else while holding the end of the leash. You can even coax him to jump up and take the snack off the counter. When he goes for the food, shake the penny can once, say "No!" and then guide him into a sit, using the leash, and say "Good boy."

The leash also enables you to reinforce the behavior you want, which is to have your dog "Sit," then praise him. The shake of the penny can creates a sudden loud noise that signals your dog not to engage in that behavior.

Caution on penny-can use: Gauge the temperament of your dog. The loud noise of the penny can does not faze some dogs, but may create other issues, such as spot peeing, in shy dogs. **Please use discretion when applying the penny-can correction.** If you own a shy or submissive dog, do not use the penny-can technique. A simple firm "No!" will suffice. It is important not to overuse the penny can. Shake the can only once and say a firm "No!" Note carefully the specific guidelines that are given for each penny-can correction in this chapter.

Bone to Pick: Spot Peeing

This behavior stems from a combination of factors: a lack of boundaries from puppyhood (either no formal training or no gating) and an extremely submissive puppy combined with an extroverted owner. The energetic, intense reactions of the owner and too much space given to an insecure puppy can cause misunderstandings and confusion for the dog. It is unclear to the dog whether the intensity coming at him is for being good or bad. This confusion creates a neurotic reaction, which makes a very submissive dog urinate.

Many people feel that spot peeing is indicative of abuse in a rescued dog or a puppy's early development. This is not necessarily the case. Some people are innately more fearful than others, carrying with them phobias and neurotic responses. So are some dogs. Again, this behavior may arise when an extremely submissive dog is raised in too much space with not enough boundaries. Regardless of the dog's past, the solution to spot peeing is the same. Spot peeing is not gender specific, but is most common in female dogs.

Dog owners tend to overcompensate for their dog's shy behavior by saying "Hi" in an intense way, especially after being gone all day. Some owners lack sensitivity to the nature of this shyness and reprimand spot peeing by yelling "No!" from across the room, only adding to their dog's stress. A guest greeting your dog can also trigger spot peeing at home. This is especially true if your guest is physically big or has a particularly dominant or high-spirited air.

Note: Check with your veterinarian to make sure that frequent urination is not due to an infection or incontinence.

People Training

You need to be aware of how to approach your dog after being absent for a long time. The intensity of saying hello to your dog is very strong after you've been away eight hours, while your dog has been snoozing. As hard as this may sound, you need to ignore your dog for the first five minutes, with no eye contact. Do not speak to him. Don't project any emotion, just nonchalantly check your answering machine and do your thing. For many dog owners, this can be difficult. You feel you are being mean to your dog. You are not being mean, just calm. With little eye contact, silently approach your dog, put on its leash, and guide the dog "Outside" to go to the bathroom. Only after your dog has gone to the bathroom, say "Hi" in a mellow way.

If spot peeing is an issue when guests visit, gate your dog prior to your guest's arrival. Ask your guests to ignore your dog when they enter your house. Ask them not to give the dog any eye contact or verbal praise. Your dog will be socialized to the sounds of guests in the house without feeling threatened. After approximately twenty minutes, guide your dog from the gated area on a leash and allow him to sniff your guest. Continue socializing with your guest, ignoring your dog. Your guest can occasionally pat the dog gently in a nonchalant way. The pattern of spot peeing should disappear as you implement this new way of socializing your dog.

Bone to Pick: Fear Biting

Fear biting is an unpredictable defensive response to anything the dog finds threatening. Most likely, it will be a fast nip directed at guests, other dogs, or children. There is often no provocation prior to a dog's behaving this way. The reaction is not a dominant attack. The bite is generated out of fear and is a defensive reaction by a insecure dog. Fear-biting dogs are generally submissive in temperament and, due to a lack of boundaries and training, become wayward.

If your dog has bitten someone, you need to call a private trainer and have the trainer work with you and your dog at home. This is potentially dangerous behavior that must be addressed and changed, not dismissed.

Senior dog parents who's mature dog has not been well socialized around children should be especially cautious when grandchildren come to visit.

Almost 80 percent of all dog bites that occur in the home come from this type of behavior. Most people visualize the "biting dog" as only a dominant, aggressive dog, certainly not their cute, shy dog called Fluffy. This is why the majority of dog bites are not reported, because they come from average pets. This is not a breed-specific issue. However, many of the small to medium breeds, such as Yorkie, Lhasa Apso, Cocker Spaniel, and Jack Russell, are the surprising culprits. Owners of many of these breeds do not formally train them, thereby leaving their dogs to fend for themselves.

Remember, behaviors take time to develop and correct. A potential fear biter can be a very sweet dog by nature—hence the unpredictability. However, there are warning signs. Your dog's tail will tell the tale. A dog who is fearful will tuck his tail between his legs. See if your dog has any of the following behavior traits that can be potential signs of fear biting.

Doggy Sign Language: Signs of a Potential Fear Biter

• Does your dog often back away from guests or people he doesn't know very well?

• Does your dog hide underneath furniture with its tail tucked, every time a child or adult guest greets him?

• Is your dog unpredictably territorial over bones, toys, or food in a snarling, possessive, or defensive way?

People Training

If you own a dog who has a shy personality, you need to provide your dog with—you guessed it—all of the basic obedience commands and boundaries, practiced at home. Giving your dog a way to please you by teaching him basic obedience will enhance your dog's trust and promote his sense of security.

Not every shy dog is a biter, but dog owners can avoid fear bites by being aware. Do not go into dog-owner denial. Symptoms are subtle and owners unintentionally compound this submissive behavior by coaxing and coddling or ignoring the reaction of a dog that is showing signs of trouble. Giving a shy or aloof dog too much freedom in your house creates a defensive reaction to anything that may scare it. This intensifies the insecurity level of an already submissive dog and allows the dog owner to overlook warning signs. If your dog has displayed any of the above signs, I offer four training tips that may help you prevent fear biting.

Four Steps to Prevent Fear Biting from a Shy Dog

1. First and foremost, you should train your dog on a leash and review "Heel," "Sit," "Stay," "Down," and "Come." See also Chapter 5, "Creating Positive Boundaries." These techniques provide you and your dog with a foundation of communication that leads to trust, no matter how shy or small your dog. Often owners of toy

and small breeds do not formally train their dogs until the dogs have bitten someone.

2.   Gate your dog before guests arrive, so the pup does not feel threatened. In addition, you need to create some structure in your dog's daily routine, designating gating time and free time.

3.   Acclimate your dog to its area gradually, always guiding him in on a leash. This technique takes away the need to coax a really shy dog. Gate your dog twenty minutes before guests arrive and keep him gated for the entire visit. This way your dog is already in its safe area and has no need to get defensive and back away from anyone.

Remember, you need to set the rules. Allowing your dog to run loose and display introverted or territorial behavior with guests only creates a pattern that may lead to a nip in the future. Gating allows your dog to build confidence over time and become socialized, without feeling threatened. Do not feel as though this is a prison for your dog. By gating him, you are being a good dog parent, providing him with a safe haven so he does not have to act out his fears.

4.   Have your guest approach the gate with a treat. If your dog is so shy that he does not approach the gate and sit for the treat, then that's all right. Have the visitor drop the treat into the gated area, and try again on another occasion. In time, your dog will become more sociable, provided you give him reassurance through use of the leash and boundaries established through gating. Obedience training is a must, and will ultimately give this type of dog the confidence it needs.

 PAW PRINT: The first canine space cadet, a Russian dog named Laika, was launched into space in 1957.

Bone to Pick: Dog Aggression

Dominance is a natural occurrence in the doggy world. We dog parents usually are the only ones who insist that our dogs get along with all other dogs. One of the ways that dogs express dominance is what I call the doggy dominance dance, commonly known as humping. This is where one dog puts his head over the other dog's shoulders in an attempt to mount him. This is not a cute hug or just a mating ritual. Although this dance does not always result in a fight, the wrong combination of dogs testing each other is sure to constitute a challenge if one of them does not back down.

The problem often presents itself in the ever-growing population at our cities' dog parks. The unneutered, mature male dog gets confronted by the unneutered, young and frisky male dog and neither one wants to submit. When dominant dogs hit maturity they often try to assert their control over certain dogs. If the other dog is older or not tolerant of this behavior, a fight happens. There is nothing worse than going to the park on a beautiful day and finding yourself praying you don't run into any other dogs because it could lead to a fight. In most cases, with proper correction and guidance during the early signs of dog aggression, the behavior will never get to an antisocial level.

Other signs of dominance are eye contact and prey drive—a movement-oriented urge to chase and catch. Prey drive is not always associated with aggressive dominance. Dogs that have a high prey drive usually need some sort of structure to their upbringing or else their energy can turn delinquent, if their needs are not met. Again, if you know your high-powered dog gets a little testy with other dogs, then when he focuses keenly on another dog and begins a high-pitched whine, this does not always mean he wants to go play. This whine stems from anxiety, which over time and mishandled by owners can contribute to possible dog aggression. You need to be able to curb this overzealous behavior before it turns into bullying.

Dog aggression has to do with a dog's natural dominance combined with a lack of training and socialization. Dog aggression can develop in any breed and in any combination of male or female dogs and can reach different degrees.

**A dominant dog does not automatically become
aggressive. If a dog does not receive the proper
education and boundaries it needs from its owner, then
a dominant disposition can develop into aggressive
tendencies.**

People Training

As a dog parent, you generally know early on whether you have a dominant puppy. If you own a dominant dog, male or female, it does not mean you are automatically going to have behavioral problems. Dogs with a moderately dominant disposition can make the best obedience dogs. It just means they need early guidance and more direction from you. Do not go into dog owner denial at the first sign of trouble. It generally indicates there is more to come.

Signs of trouble appear slowly during adolescence and on into maturity. Bullying other dogs, possessiveness with toys, and guarding territories (like your front door and backyard) become the telltale signs. Obedience training on a leash in and around these trouble spots is essential.

Your dog's tail will tell the tale. A dominant dog will carry his tail very high and erect. It is true that certain breeds are prone to having a more dominant disposition, like most guard dogs, some of the herding breeds, Chow Chows, and terriers, to name a few. However, some little dogs can be just as feisty in temperment, especially when walking on a leash. One of the first signs of dominant behavior is when your dog becomes very protective on leash, barking at other dogs across the street. Many dog owners tend to dismiss this reaction toward the odd dog and allow the barking to continue, instead of correcting it immediately. Remember, your dog wants you to be his leader.

At home, if your dog has access to a window facing the street and rushes to the window, barking furiously, this is a sign of potential dog aggression. This form of dominance is unacceptable, although common. Another household area that fuels overly dominant behavior is a fenced yard that faces the street, if your dog has access to guard his territory. If a dog that is kept in a backyard the greater part of the time can see other dogs and people on the street, many unwanted behaviors can result.

As a dog owner you need to take certain precautions, such as training, early neutering, and socialization. Extreme dog aggression is usually not seen in young pups. If you see it in yours, then you should call a professional trainer immediately. Just as with people, there are some completely antisocial dogs.

How to Prevent Dog Aggression

1.   *Neuter your dog early.* If you live in an area with a large population of dogs and your lifestyle requires you to have a well-socialized dog, neuter your dog. Neutering a male dog early in adolescence will help prevent a dominant temperament from becoming an aggressive one in maturity. Once a behavior has already begun, neutering alone will not eliminate the behavior, but you should still have it done. Seek a professional trainer for additional help.

2.   *Train and socialize him.* If your instincts say that your puppy is on the dominant side, then you need to train him early on and socialize him a lot. It would be a good idea to invest in an advanced obedience class. Applying all of the obedience commands within your daily routine will reinforce the guidance your dog needs.

3.   *Use exercise to take off the edge.* An Alpha, or dominant, puppy usually has high prey and play drives. If his exercise needs do not get met, then the energy often turns into anxiety and frustration, which can lead to aggression if not averted by you.

4.   *Watch for the doggy dominance dance, also known as humping.* If your dog often begins the dominance dance in parks, you can correct him or her and say "No!" If he begins to growl, put him on a leash and give a quick sharp correction with a tug of the leash, saying a firm "No!" and begin a quick "Heel." This diverts his attention from the dominance dance to what you want him to do. You must assert your will in a kind and confident way. Think Mary Poppins with an edge. Be firm with the correction but pleasant with the command.

5.   *Prevent the embarrassment that comes from owning the neighborhood bully.* Having a guard dog is one thing, but owning the neighborhood

menace is another. To stop excessive barking from behind a fence, give a firm shake of the penny can from a distance and say "No!" Change your dog's pattern by not allowing obsessive barking to begin. Use foresight and gate your dog inside with a chew bone when neighborhood dogs are being walked at the end of the work day.

Never tie up your dog at any time. This creates frustration and anxiety and will cause aggression in time.

People Training

Mild dog aggression can begin slowly without your even realizing it. Allowing your dog to bark at other dogs while on a walk can lead to more serious behavior over time. Dog aggression usually progresses because of a combination of the above elements all going uncorrected. The following four steps help you prevent your dog from barking at other dogs while walking on a leash.

1. Practice heeling using a training collar and a leash.

2. Use quick sharp snaps of the collar to indicate the intended speed of your walk. Say "Heel" repeatedly, in a pleasant voice.

3. As you see another dog across the street and before your dog begins to bark, say No! with a quick snap of the leash.

4. Quickly pivot in the opposite direction from the other dog and keep walking, while telling your dog to "Heel." Keep saying "Heel" with many quick snaps of the leash and keep walking.

What often happens to people as they confront another dog on a walk is that they, and their dog, get distracted. Once your dog has begun to bark at the other dog, the human reaction is to just hold on for dear life and say "NO!" a lot, instead of diverting your dog's attention off the other dog and onto a positive command, such as "Heel."

The next time you confront another dog while walking, your dog will attempt the same behavior, but now you will know how to nip it in the bud.

Bone to Pick: Barking like a Maniac at Other Dogs from the Car
Does this sound familiar? You're driving along with the car window down and your dog's ears are flapping in the wind. You stop at a red light and out of the corner of your eye you see a woman walking her Schnauzer. Your worst nightmare is about to become real. You scramble to roll up your windows when your dog begins to bark, making a noise similar to that of a machine gun. You attempt to say "No!" but the only beings that hear you are the people in the cars next to you and on the street. Mostly, you're hoping the light will change.

This common problem is also a sign of potential dog aggression. Some dogs go nuts because they are movement-oriented and their prey drive is so acute that the fast motion of cars stimulates them to bark, others bark to protect the territory of their car. This behavior is most prevalent among adult dogs two years of age and up. It is due mostly to territorialism and excitement. However, it *must* be stopped. If your dog rides in a car infrequently, this could also add to the behavior.

People Training
Try this four-part technique.

1. Keep a penny can in the front seat of your car.

2. Do a test ride with your dog around the block.

3. If he starts barking, shake the can once and say "No!" He might begin barking again. Shake it again once, saying "No!" The sudden noise will startle your dog and give him a clear signal that the barking is not okay and that you mean business.

4. The barking might happen again during the next car ride, but if you keep using this technique the problem will go away eventually.

 PAW PRINT: There is only one breed of dog in the world that does not bark. It is the Basenji.

Bone to Pick: Digging to China

Coming home after a nice afternoon of shopping and finding a giant hole in your newly manicured lawn can be infuriating. Digging is usually a habit that develops during the teenage stage of your pup's development. It is a common hobby of many pampered pooches. Some dogs are diggers and some are not. There are many reasons why dogs dig, but the main reason most dogs dig stems from boredom. Many people get upset when they hear this reason and begin reciting a laundry list of toys they have bought and time that they spend with their pups. What I mean by boredom is a lack of socialization. Too many hours spent in a backyard on a daily basis, or not enough social interaction on walks, can constitute a lack of socialization.

People Training

Dogs that spend endless hours in a backyard daily generally go through a phase of digging. Giving your dog a bone to chew outdoors often entices some dogs to bury the treat for later enjoyment. You can break a dog's habit with more walks and less time in the yard. Most dogs grow out of this phase. However, the following tips can help detour your dog's urge to dig.

• Limit your dog's time in the backyard to playing fetch with you.

• If you do give your dog backyard time alone, make sure that he has been exercised first. The playing should tire him and thus curb his desire to dig.

• Do not allow your dog to chew bones or pig's ears in the backyard. The temptation to bury them could become overwhelming.

• Give your dog tennis balls and other hard rubber toys to play with in the backyard. This will encourage him to play rather than dig.

Working out the kinks requires patience, consistency, and follow-through on YOUR part. Choosing the right canine companion in the first place is crucial to your success. Your disposition and your dog's temperament must match. If they don't, and you are not able to meet your dog's needs or fit them into your lifestyle, that is when the kinks will show.

Remember that the original breed purpose needs to be re-searched by you so that you have an idea of where your dog's innate drives come from. This awareness will prevent many kinks from developing. For instance, if you own an Australian cattle dog that has been bred to herd sheep, you know that while this dog is young he will need to have plenty of exercise and training from you. If he doesn't get it, that energy could turn into excessive bark-ing, or the destruction of your things.

All dogs need to bond. The way to bond with a dog is to praise him while he is obeying a command. This gives your dog a solid way to please you and makes him feel loved. Training allows for that connection to take place.

At Your Service

Youth will be served, every dog has his
day, and mine has been a fine one.
—GEORGE BORROW

Pet services have become very popular. Choosing a dog walker, a
health insurance plan, or a boarding kennel can confuse any dog
parent because there are so many options. Within the first six
months of owning your new pooch you may be asking a lot of
questions about pet care. Going out of town for a weekend suddenly becomes a critical maneuver. What is the best thing to do
with your new best friend when you go on vacation? How do you
research and find the right kennel facility? How do you find a good
group training class, or veterinarian?

In this chapter I offer guidelines to help ease the confusion
when you are searching for the best pet services in your town. The
chapter concludes with some advice on traveling with your dog.

VETERINARIAN

Location is really important in finding the right veterinarian for
you. For the first year of his life, your puppy will need a series of

puppy shots, so having a vet at a convenient location is helpful. Prices for puppy shots, neutering, and spaying can vary among vets, so call around.

Your veterinarian can also be a great reference for other service providers such as local groomers, trainers, and kennels in your area. Upon getting your new best friend, ask your vet about vaccination clinics and spay and neutering clinics that offer services at reduced rates.

You might want to get *The Dog Owner's Home Veterinary Handbook* by Delbert G. Carlson, D.V.M., and James M. Giffin, M.D. (Howell, 1992), to familiarize yourself with all aspects of dog health care.

Your puppy's vaccination schedule is important. Ensuring your dog's future health means not allowing the vaccination schedule to lapse. Make sure your puppy gets the complete series of puppy shots to build adequate amounts of antibodies in its system to fight off viruses and possible diseases. The following series of shots helps to build up puppies' immune systems to fight off infectious diseases.

Puppy Shot Timetable

6–8 weeks.................Canine distemper-measles-parainfluenza (CPI) parvovirus
8–12 weeks...............DHLPP (distemper, hepatitis, leptospirosis, parainfluenza, parvovirus) coronavirus and rabies at 12 weeks
16 weeks...................DHLPP, coronavirus
12 months.................Rabies
Annual booster.........DHLPP, coronavirus, rabies (booster lasting one or three years, as your veterinarian recommends)

<u>Note:</u> The best age to spay or neuter your dog is between six and eight months. However, check with your vet. One thing for sure, it is never too late to fix your dog. There are overwelming numbers of unwanted puppies and dogs in our shelters. Please, take responsiblity and spay or neuter your dog.

PET HEALTH INSURANCE

Pet health insurance is a preventive, protective, and worthwhile measure. Many dog owners are not familiar with health insurance for dogs. Even my response was guarded. "Health insurance for my dog? I'm not sure, I'll think about it."

After the initial expense of getting a puppy, spending more money for this preventive measure was not foremost in my mind. A few years later, because of accidents, I wished I had gotten pet health insurance. My German Shepherd Bo was a healthy four-year-old when he severed the ligament that holds the knee together. The extent of his injury was not apparent for several months despite many vet visits. A chronic limp that started after exercise was first diagnosed as a sprain and then possible arthritis.

After several different opinions based on X rays and other tests, and months of painkillers, Bo had to undergo cruciate ligament surgery costing thousands of dollars. Although this is a common sports injury to human athletes, I never thought it could happen to my German Shepherd. After this long and expensive lesson, I now advocate looking into health insurance for your pet. You never know what's going to happen over the life span of your pet—on average, ten to fifteen years. Pet health insurance operates much like human health-care plans.

What you need to know about health insurance for your dog:

• Statistically, two out of three dogs experience major medical problems in their lifetime.

• Most pet health insurance companies let you select any vet, specialist, or hospital.

• Many pet health insurance companies insure puppies eight weeks of age and up.

• Rates are usually based on age of the pet and the selected plan, averaging $100 per year and up.

• Most pet insurance companies have plans that cover routine office visits, spaying and neutering costs, teeth cleaning, and minor ailments such as skin and ear problems, as well as accidents and major illnesses.

Ask your local veterinarian about more information and literature regarding health insurance companies.

Having foresight and buying health insurance for their dog can be a solution for dog owners who perhaps cannot afford expensive treatments and would face tough choices if a serious health problem came up. As your pup matures, your vet bill can add up to thousands of dollars, and insurance is a wise form of protection.

GROUP TRAINING CLASSES

Group dog training is an inexpensive way to socialize and bond with your dog, provided you find a good trainer. It is, however, important to ask for references. Any good trainer should have tons of former students who would love to tell you how successful the training methods were.

The best way to find a good group training class is to ask your veterinarian. She or he should be able to recommend a reputable trainer. Use your instincts: If you don't like the trainer as a person, you will not learn from him or her. Training should make sense to you and also be fun.

For other dog-related activities and classes it is always a great idea to check out local all-breed dog shows in your area. Upcoming dog shows, which often include obedience trials and agility events, are usually listed in local newspapers. Or you can call the American Kennel Club and ask for a schedule of shows in your area.

If you are interested in hiring a private dog trainer to solve behavioral issues, make sure the training is done in your home rather than in a kennel. Sending your dog away to be trained is not a good idea. Your dog needs to be trained in his own environment and you need to be a part of the process.

PAW PRINT: The first three AKC obedience championships were all won by Golden Retrievers.

Tips for Picking a Group Class

• Class size should be a maximum of ten dogs with their owners.

• The teacher should work with each dog.

• You should ask for a written course outline to learn what will be covered before committing to the class.

Make sure your puppy is at least four months old and has all of its shots.

DOG WALKERS

Dog walker? To many this service sounds rather pretentious. Whether you need a dog walker largely depends on your routine, where you live, and the age of your dog. However, if you live in an urban area, work, and own a dog, a walker can be a lifesaver on busy days. This is especially true if you have a young pup that thinks he is the Energizer rabbit, and you have already had a twelve-hour day. Most dog walkers charge by the hour, and employing one is a relatively inexpensive present to yourself. Your needs may vary from week to week, and a walker could be helpful in those busy weeks. Ask your local kennel owner, veterinarian, or groomer for possible dog walkers and pet-sitting services. The word of mouth around pet-oriented businesses is usually reliable. The following are a few guidelines for choosing the right dog walker for you.

• Ask for references.

• Know that a reputable dog walker should be bonded. It is important that your pooch gets out of the house or apartment, but it's also important that your jewelry stays in!

• Make sure the walker exercises your dog, not just walks him. Some of the dog walkers I have interviewed even take Polaroid pictures of their clients' dogs during hikes and at play with other dogs. This helps reassure the dog parents that their dogs' needs are actually being met.

 PAW PRINT: The Irish Wolfhound is the tallest recognized breed of dog in the world.

DOGGY ACUPUNCTURE

Acupuncture for dogs? Believe it or not, acupuncture is becoming popular in many veterinary practices. Acupuncture is a form of traditional Chinese medicine that helps stimulate and balance the immune system. The only downside is that it can get to be rather costly over a long period of time. Ask your local veterinarian about any holistic veterinary clinics in your area, and whether this treatment may be right for your dog. It's an option you may want to consider.

Acupuncture and acupressure use opiates that are produced naturally in a dog's body to kill pain and sedate nerves. Acupuncture works via the placement of needles at specific energy points, depending on the particular ailment being treated. Acupressure calls for the application of pressure instead of needles to energy points. Both procedures are used to treat dogs that suffer from skin allergies, arthritis, painful bone disorders, paralysis, hip dysplasia, and irritable bowel disease. People generally pursue acupuncture for their dogs when nothing else works.

TAIL WAG: J.D. SOUTHER

My client J.D. Souther, songwriter for The Eagles, Linda Ronstadt, Trisha Yearwood, Don Henley, and others gives his two rescued dogs, Baby Girl and Murphy, the best of his love when it comes to their health. J.D. discovered the benefits of acupuncture when treatments helped prevent possible surgery on his own knee.

He wondered what effect it would have on his dogs. Baby Girl, a beautiful Doberman mix, was prone to occasional pulled muscles, due to an old back injury. Murphy, a spaniel mix, woke up one day having no control over his back legs. After doing research, J.D. brought both dogs to a renowned Los Angeles acupunture clinic for animals. Murphy was treated for a pinched nerve in his leg. Luckily, the acupuncture treatments revived the nerve in Murphy's leg and also alleviated the pain in Baby Girl's hip.

J.D. is very grateful that acupuncture got to the "Heart of the Matter,"* without surgery for his pets.

*Song written by J.D. Souther for The Eagles

KENNELS

Leaving your dog in a kennel for the first time can be stressful for both of you. Is kenneling your dog a good idea? What should you look for in a kennel?

Visit several kennels in your area in advance, unannounced, and ask for a tour. Most good kennels will comply. The following are things to consider in choosing a kennel.

- Is the kennel clean?

- Are the staff members friendly?

- Is there an exercise area?

• Ask the kennel staff what the procedure is for sick dogs. Is there an on-staff vet?

• Are there any hidden costs? Some kennels charge extra for blankets, play time, or outside walks; for administering medications; or even if your dog exceeds a certain weight. Ask for an estimate for your dog's proposed length of stay. (Bathing is usually an extra cost. It is wise to schedule grooming for the last day of the kennel stay.)

• Ask about the kennel's feeding procedures. Is there only a limited variety of kibble? If your dog is on a special diet that the kennel does not offer, there will probably be an extra charge for feeding your dog different food. Remember, it is important to feed your dog the same dog food that he gets at home while he is in a kennel. Sudden diet changes could upset his stomach.

• Ask if the kennel has someone on site around the clock, in case of emergencies.

To ease your guilt about kenneling your dog, remember that while being boarded in a kennel your dog experiences an enormous amount of stimulation. Contrary to popular belief, your dog is getting a great deal of socialization by being away from home. At kennels, there is the excitement of new people cleaning, exercising, and feeding the dog. There is rarely a dull moment.

Initially many dogs experience stress going into a kennel. To help alleviate tension, make sure the dog run your pooch is going to be kept in has some sort of paneling or opaque partition, so your dog has an area to relax privately.

I recommend kenneling your dog, provided you find a good kennel and like the people who are running it. However, kenneling your dog for lengthy stays is not advisable. Some dogs will suffer from depression if their owner is gone too long. A brief kennel stay of a week or so can be fun for dogs and give you peace of mind.

CAR RIDES

For many dogs, their second car ride ends up being a trip to the vet. Conditioning your pup to ride in the car should start at an early age with short trips to the park, not just the vet's office. If you want a new pup to be relaxed in the car, you will need to acclimate him.

Some pups are natural car dogs, loving the experience. Others are sensitive to sounds and movement and get carsick. If your dog gets carsick, know it will probably grow out of this phase as it matures. Sometimes carsickness can be due to an inner ear problem. Check with your veterinarian. You can begin getting your pup used to being in the car by taking only very small trips. Do not feed your dog prior to a car ride. Begin with around the block and the following week take your dog on a quick car ride to a park. Try to associate each short trip with a positive experience. Socialize him slowly to experiencing car rides as fun, and as he matures he should grow out of the motion sickness.

If your dog is a wild child in the car, bouncing from seat to seat, a helpful tip is to tire him out before the car ride. Your rides to the park are actually creating this rambunctious behavior because your dog is anticipating the park. The best advice is to condition your dog slowly by using foresight and taking him on short trips. Change the route you take to the park, or take him to a different park occasionally. Any pattern change will help modify this behavior.

Caution
Never leave your dog unattended in your car. During the summer months' hot temperatures, your dog can get heat stroke in minutes, and this may possibly lead to death.

LONG-DISTANCE CAR TRIPS

Remember, cars get better gas mileage on long trips. You may have to stop more often for your dog than for gas.

Road Trip Checklist

- Make sure you take a dog bowl and plenty of bottled water.

- Pack your dog's regular food. Changing your dog's diet suddenly can cause a major stomach upset.

- Make sure all name tags are legible and dog tags are current.

- Purchase a temporary name tag (sold in pet stores). This is an inexpensive way to ensure your pet's safety while in a new location. Write the address and phone number of the place you are staying and put it on your dog's collar along with his regular identification.

- Pack your dog's bed or a familiar blanket to help him relax at your destination.

- If you have a young dog, make sure you take plenty of chew bones and toys to keep him entertained at your destination.

- If your dog is an adolescent and not totally trustworthy, take a baby gate or crate with you in order to socialize him comfortably in a new place.

- Exercise your dog before a long car trip.

- Make sure you keep your dog on a leash during pit stops.

 PAW PRINT: Lapdogs were popular flea repellents in the Middle Ages. By carrying a dog around, the fleas were supposedly attracted to the dog, leaving its owner flea free.

AIRLINE TRAVEL WITH YOUR DOG

When flying with Fido, you must do your research and prepare your dog psychologically. The first time you fly with your dog you are both stressed. You read the articles on how dogs get lost and wonder if you are doing the right thing. You find out upon calling the airlines that your dog has to be small enough to fit beneath the seat in front of you, otherwise he must fly in the lower deck with the baggage. You begin to feel guilty that your best friend is now being considered cargo. Don't worry. The following guidelines will help you and your pooch have a good flight.

Flight Preparation Checklist

• Buy a crate that meets airline regulations and in which your dog can comfortably turn around and lie down.

• If your dog is not conditioned to a crate or sky kennel, begin acclimating him in advance slowly, over a period of several weeks. Set up a crate with the door open during the day while you are home for a couple of hours. Encourage your dog to chew a bone in the crate and hang out like he used to when he was a puppy. Later, increase the time to all night and close the crate door while you are sleeping. This teaches your dog to relax for long periods of time.

• If your dog is accustomed to a crate, prepare for the trip by having him spend a few hours a day in the crate with the crate door closed a week prior to your trip. This will give your dog a security blanket, and you, peace of mind.

• Make sure that you can buy your brand of dog food at your destination. It is not a good idea to switch dog food on your pup while traveling; therefore make suitable arrangements prior to travel.

Tips for Airline Travel

• Call your airline in advance. Make sure your sky kennel or canine carrier meets airline standards before you fly. Check prices and individual carrier rules and regulations. Be sure they have space for your dog.

• Make sure the baggage compartment that your pet will be kept in is heated and *pressurized*.

• Don't travel until your dog is at least eight weeks old and fully weaned.

• Call your vet and get a health certificate for your dog. Some airlines require a health certificate thirty days in advance.

• Keep the health certificate with your other travel documents because you will need it traveling home as well.

• Ask your vet if you should sedate your dog prior to flying. Some dogs are very anxious and a tranquilizer may make the experience easier.

• Airline fees vary depending on the individual airline carrier and the weight of your dog. Call ahead to know the charges.

• Many overseas destinations have restrictions on pets, requiring your dog to remain in quarantine for up to six months. For instance, England and Hawaii have a six-month quarantine, whereas France has none.

• Ask the airlines in advance about temperature restrictions during the summer and winter months. If the temperature is above or below a certain reading, many airlines will not fly pets.

Pre-boarding

• Do not feed your dog for six hours before the flight.

• Make sure he has gone to the bathroom prior to the flight.

• Water can spill out of the sky kennel's small serving cup. It is best to fill the cups with water and freeze them overnight. On the day of travel, the ice will thaw slowly. Another idea is to get a water bottle that dispenses water slowly, like the kind used for rabbits.

• Make sure that your dog is wearing ID tags. Write all information including your address and phone number and the destination on the sky kennel. Most airlines have "Live Animal" stickers to place on the outside of the kennel, too.

• Upon boarding, if the airline does not provide a check-in system confirming that your dog has made it onto the plane, ask the flight attendant for confirmation. Make sure you confirm that your pooch made it onto the flight safely. Have a good trip!

Whether you are flying, driving, or kenneling your pup, I hope the information in this chapter will assist you and encourage your reasearch into the pet services available in your neighborhood.

But before you pack up your family for that road trip, find out how to have it all—the home, the kids, the dog—and keep your sanity.

CHAPTER

13

Having It All:
The Home,
the Kids, the Dog

> There is my opinion, there is your
> opinion, and then there's the truth.
> —ANONYMOUS

Human nature is such that, driven by wanting it all, we often bite off more than we can chew. That is what happens in families that have small children and busy schedules, and get a young puppy.

We are inundated with messages that constantly confirm the ease of having it all. We all aspire to it, and we know there are few things more amazing than the face of a child who is holding a new puppy for the first time. Sometimes, however, our vision of Lassie can turn into a Stephen King plot if we are not prepared to take full responsibility.

The preparation needed for raising a dog and a family includes a realistic assessment of who the new puppy's main caretaker will be. Parents who are not dog lovers themselves should simply not get a dog for their children. The most difficult combination to manage is toddler and puppy. It is my humble recommendation that you not get a dog until your children are at least five years old. Teething puppies and children in diapers do not mix well. You will become a referee and a sanitation engineer and possibly end up resenting the puppy because you feel overwhelmed.

Many of us have selective memory when it comes to raising a dog. When we think back to our childhood experiences, it seems that the messes miraculously got cleaned, the dog fed, and the furniture remained intact. Living with a new puppy again can be a wake-up call. Therefore, it's crucial that at least one parent be a dog lover, willing to take full charge of raising, training, and walking the family dog.

This chapter will cover the basic concerns that every parent has with introducing their old dog to a new baby, and tips on how to survive the toddler stage with both your child and your puppy. The scenarios and tips will teach parents how to manage raising a young puppy and find a fun way to include older children into the process. Having it all requires patience, consistency, and lots of positive reinforcement. These are the same ingredients that both you and your pooch need for training.

Parents' Golden Rules on Pups and Kids

1.   Do not expect your child to be the primary caretaker of a new puppy. You need to set an example for both your child and your dog.

2.   Teach your children how to be gentle with their new pet.

3.   Set a scheduled playtime for your children with their new pup.

- Tire your new puppy first and then designate a supervised playtime of fifteen minutes. Puppies get rambunctious. If you exercise the pup first he will be calmer when he plays with your children.

- Make sure the puppy has eliminated before playtime.

4.   Always gate your dog when there are a number of children around. It is always better to be safe than sorry. Even if your dog is good with kids, it doesn't mean all kids are good with your dog.

5.   Do not allow a small child to be around your puppy without supervision when the pup has a bone or food.

6.   Teach your children never to run up to strange dogs.

7.   Show your child how to pat a dog, not hug or squeeze.

I know that it can be challenging to keep very young children at bay with a new puppy, but that is why gating young puppies in their own area at specific times is helpful. Children need to be taught by you how to be gentle with dogs of any age. A good way to teach young children is to create a game using a stuffed animal. Show your child where the puppy's eyes, nose, mouth, and tail are on the stuffed animal. Then carefully teach your child not to poke the eyes or pull a dog's ears or tail. Reinforce how to caress a puppy the right way.

In addition, it is important for parents to tell their children why a puppy needs to chew and bark, so that they don't misinterpret natural functions of a dog and become fearful. The above points are crucial for all parents to note. Too many unnecessary accidents happen because of a lack of foresight on the part of the adult. Just as you child-proof your house for a toddler, there are ways of child-proofing your pooch. It is a good idea for all parents to do this with their puppy or even an older dog.

Whether you own an old faithful friend or a new puppy, know that children between the ages of twelve months and five years with a dog often need to be supervised. You might need to invest in referee clothes and a whistle. A toddler and a puppy together— look out! Children can thoughtlessly hit, poke, pull fur, and squeeze the dog. Even when done affectionately, it is a lot to expect a dog to put up with.

Child-Proofing Your Pooch

•   Teach your pup early that nothing is his and everything is yours. Put your hands in your dog's food dish while he is eating and hand-feed him a couple handfuls of food.

- Hold a bone while he is chewing it. While you are watching TV, hold on to the bone your puppy is chewing for a few minutes. This gets him used to sharing his bone with others.

- Practice touching your pup's feet. This helps your pup understand that he can be touched without being hurt and it builds trust. It also prepares him for when he gets his nails clipped during grooming.

- While your puppy is relaxed, gently pull on its tail—not in a hurtful way, of course.

These actions simulate what young children might do to pups. It is important to introduce these movements to your puppy beforehand, so he doesn't react in a defensive manner in the future.

When you and your partner find out you are going to have a baby, it's time to think about how you will present the new bundle of joy to the one with the big ears and tail. Depending on your dog's temperament and your circumstances, there are things you can do to make the transition easier for both you and your dog at the time of your baby's arrival.

How Do I Prepare My Old Dog for the New Baby?

Since having a baby represents a major change in your life, it also affects your dog. It is difficult to summarize all the variables involved in introducing a mature dog to an infant. Each dog has a distinct temperament and many issues involve a particular home environment. However, there are some basic guidelines.

Assuming there are no serious issues to address, such as aggression, which would require behavior modification, preparing your dog entails the following. Put your dog, no matter what age, on a routine to prepare for the coming changes. This routine includes gating, exercise, and training, so that when the baby arrives, and you have less time for the dog, he can get accustomed to the smells and noises of this new creature in the house while safely gated.

While you are at home, give your dog a special bone or chew toy in his gated area. This teaches your dog that he has his own space, and takes away the potential for territorialism to happen. Gate him for twenty-minute increments, beginning months before your baby is due. Gating your dog in a designated area, one that is not isolated, allows the dog to den. Do not feel bad; this is not a punishment. The den will give him a sense of security while the household changes.

Reviewing all of the basic commands with him is always a good idea. It reinforces a pecking order for the household that makes you the leader. Do some on-leash training in the new baby's room to make your dog feel included and loved. In the midst of such a radical shift in the family as having a baby, your dog senses hormone-level and mood changes, and these sometimes give him mixed signals. He may become more protective. Even if your dog is your golden child, the fact that you are bringing a new child home can leave the dog feeling very insecure. The day you bring your baby home, gate the dog prior to your arrival. Gating the dog also prevents surprise behaviors from developing.

If your dog exhibits any severe behavioral abnormalities like growling, showing his teeth, or attempting to bite a visitor or family member, call a dog trainer immediately.

We Wanted Lassie and Got Jaws

The number one question I get asked by parents with young children and puppies is, "How do I stop my puppy from jumping up and nipping my child?" It is not uncommon that a four-month old puppy and a six-year old child can't seem to be in the same room together without someone being in tears. Parents must remember nipping and jumping is only a stage in their puppy's development. Reprimanding this behavior is like asking your toddler to sit still at a formal dinner party. No matter how much you reprimand or explain, it is not going to happen.

Puppies that are teething need to chew, and some puppies' teething periods are worse than others. It is better to avert the whole situation by exhausting the puppy through exercise and then allowing your children to pat and cuddle him.

The way puppies play with one another is by biting and tumbling. The way your children play with the puppy can stimulate that very same biting and tumbling urge. The pup sees your child as a playmate and wants to wrestle, which means biting and nipping. Again, I would not try to reprimand this. I would separate them.

Dogs perceive children as submissive rather than dominant, treating them like littermates, not pack leaders. What's more, young children generally cannot offer dogs the guidance they need because of their own inconsistency. Therefore it is unrealistic to rely on a child to formally guide and manage his or her dog, even on a leash, without your leadership and instruction.

Guess what, parents? You need to know that whatever your child's age, you are the main caretaker of the new pup. Sorry. Many people get a new puppy for their children expecting them to care for and raise the dog. Parents give their kids a dog hoping the experience will teach their children responsibility. Often this form of education is at the dog's expense, and ends up in doggy divorce. Parents must remember that a five- or ten-year-old child needs direction from them. If you do not want to take care of a dog, your child will find it a chore as well, once the novelty has worn off.

Children look to their parents to take the lead (no pun intended). To expect a child to raise and care for a puppy is one guaranteed way to foster behavioral issues in the pup. Usually everyone in the family has the very best intentions. However, soccer practice and homework and friends take over. You will end up having to deal with it anyway. However, there is a way to guide everyone to participate.

CREATE A FUN "PUPPY PROJECT" FOR YOUR KIDS

The best way to introduce children five to ten years old to a puppy as a new member of the family is to set an example. Approach the process of housebreaking and training a puppy as you would teach the ABCs. A creative way to do this, and have fun with the whole family, is to make a puppy notebook. The book provides structure and personalizes the process of raising the new pup. It also helps your children gauge the pup's progress, and it becomes a fun keepsake for years to come.

Take a picture of the pup and glue it on the cover of the notebook. Inside the book, outline with great colors a feeding and potty schedule for your child to fill out on a daily basis. Children then feel as though raising the new puppy is a fun project. With your supervision, they should continue to add photos and drawings to the notebook, making a lifelong memento. It may seem like more work for you at first, but it's better than being a constant referee.

TEACHING YOUR CHILDREN TO DO OBEDIENCE TRAINING

In my experience with teaching children to train dogs, I have found that kids are good mimics. So remember, you need to set an example. If the whole family participates in the raising of a new puppy, and a good example is given, children will usually follow the lead enthusiastically. However, if the child is left alone to conquer the task of training a pet, the novelty quickly disappears. Your kids lose interest without your paricipation and you end up taking care of an unruly dog.

The best tip I can give is that the dog needs you to guide and train him first, with consistency, before children get involved. When the puppy has a good understanding of the basic commands and reaches his teens, then have your child take on some obedience training. Children six years old and up are good candidates for holding this responsibility, but only with you as their glowing example.

A six-year old can be a big help in keeping a feeding and potty schedule. Teaching your child to guide the dog on a leash around the house with your supervision is a great place to start. Have your child take a few steps while saying "Heel" and then stop and pull up on the leash while saying "Sit." Commands like "Stay," "Down," and "Come" are too advanced for a child because they require consistency.

TEACHING CHILDREN HOW TO GIVE THE DOG A TREAT

A large dog biscuit is the best treat for young children to give dogs. The treat is oversized and lessens the chance of little hands getting in the way. Plus, it takes longer for a dog to eat a large treat than a smaller one; dogs tend to devour small treats one after the next.

Children generally hold treats up in the air. This causes the dog to jump up to get it. Teach your child to hand the dog a treat. Giving a treat is obviously a great bonding exercise for everyone.

• *Big dogs and little kids:* To include your small child in the training process, try this exercise. Put a training collar and leash on your dog and stand with him on your left-hand side. Give your child a large dog biscuit. Direct your child to stand in front and say the word "Sit." As your child says the command, silently pull up on the leash and guide your dog to sit. Once the dog complies, ask your child to reach out and give the dog a treat. After several weeks of this exercise, your dog will learn to wait (not snatch the treat out of your child's hand) and to take direction from your child, with your supervision. If your dog snaps for the treat, you can correct him for lunging with a quick snap of the leash and a firm "No!" Then try again covering your child's hand and give the treat together to the dog.

• *Little dogs and big kids:* Big children tend to torment little dogs, albeit unintentionally. Accidents can happen. Many little dogs can jump high for treats, amusing most children—until someone gets bitten. Teach your child not to hold the treat too high. It is always best to ask your dog to sit for a treat before giving it to him. As for the jumping, have your kids bounce a ball outside, allowing your little dog to jump and catch the ball, instead of a hand-held treat. Parents get the treat of teaching these fun tips to their children, while eliminating the potential of big accidents. Approximately 60 percent of all dog bites are accidents involving children. The majority of dog bites are not by vicious, untrained dogs. They are accidents involving family pets.

Bone to pick: When the dog growls at kids, is he just jealous?
Be particularly aware of any interaction between your dog and neighborhood children. Children and dogs should not be unsupervised. If your dog ever growls at your child or an adult, this is not okay. It is a warning, a sign that the dog will bite—if not now, then in the future. Make sure you also take precautions, by separating

your child and dog with a baby gate, especially if there are bones and food around. A common circumstance for a dog to growl at a child occurs around food. This is not healthy behavior and should be addressed immediately.

There are too many unknown variables, such as the age and temperament of your dog or previously formed bad habits that need to be modified, for me to responsibly offer a quick correction. However, this is a signal for you to seek the help of an expert. Call a trainer immediately, before an accident happens.

Remember, it is important for a trainer or a professional behaviorist to come to your home and show you specifically how to modify this behavior, tailoring the correction to your circumstances.

Training the owner, in this case the parent, is essential. Puppies need guidance from you, as do your kids. Being a parent to your puppy and children can be challenging. However, the two can mix nicely if you set a few boundaries.

All of the parent tips I offer may initially seem like quite a bit of work, but, if followed, the advice will make your life less hectic. It is very important to teach your children and their friends to be gentle with all dogs, especially puppies. The best time to let your child play with the pup is when the pooch is exhausted. Play ball or let your pup run around and get tired first, then let your small child hang out with Lassie. By implementing the golden rules and fun games, you ensure that everyone will enjoy the new family member.

Tail's End

> You have to remember: The truth is
> funny.
> —TIMOTHY LEARY

Paws for a minute and think about this: You are on your way to having the relationship you have always wanted with your best friend. Now you realize dog training doesn't have to be boot camp, but rather is a bonding experience. Pawsing a few minutes a day with your dog will open up a great relationship.

The longer you live with your dog, the more you realize that a strange, indescribable, unconditional, and irreplaceable bond has developed. A dog has the kind of spirit that knows when you're sad, mad, or stressed and never takes it personally. Think of that family member who is always happy to see you and never gets mad at you, no matter how many hours of golf or basketball you have played. Or the one who will kiss you with or without bad breath. Or who couldn't care less how much money you earn. Training your pooch is a small payment to make for priceless rewards.

The funny thing about dogs is that unexplainable way they mirror our quirks. Whether our dogs are Dachshunds or Dobermans, we all end up as dog-and-owner lookalikes. Don't ask me how it happens, but we've all seen people walking down the street looking like the spitting image of their dogs.

I must confess my terrier and I have a similar spunk, and, on a bad hair day, I look in the rearview mirror at her while driving and laugh. When a laugh creates a tail wag it is apparent that spontaneity and unconditional love are what pups and people have in common.

The reason I wrote this book was to make training fun and a process to which people could relate.

My instruction is about teaching dog owners to have foresight, communicate clearly, and use reverse psychology to be a little smarter than their dog. The bonding between a dog parent and a pooch happens through praise during a command, not discipline. This gives your dog a solid way to please you and makes him feel loved. Training allows for this connection to take place. I hope this book has created a fun awareness of how my style of people training creates this bond, by introducing a new understanding.

So don't worry about making mistakes along the way. He'll forgive you. The greatest thing about your dog is he'll love you no matter what.

If you have more bones to chew on or tails to wag, you can contact Inger at www.pawsforaminute.com.

Index